Do-It-Yourself GUITAR

BY MICHAEL MUELLER

Video by John Heussenstamm and Tom Gillen

Audio by Doug Boduch and Jake Johnson

PLAYBACK+
Speed • Pitch • Balance • Loop

To access audio and video visit:
www.halleonard.com/mylibrary

Enter Code
7300-6592-9193-7358

ISBN 978-1-5400-9479-7

Visit Hal Leonard Online at
www.halleonard.com

Contact us:
Hal Leonard
7777 West Bluemound Road
Milwaukee, WI 53213
Email: info@halleonard.com

In Europe, contact:
Hal Leonard Europe Limited
42 Wigmore Street
Marylebone, London, W1U 2RN
Email: info@halleonardeurope.com

In Australia, contact:
Hal Leonard Australia Pty. Ltd.
4 Lentara Court
Cheltenham, Victoria, 3192 Australia
Email: info@halleonard.com.au

Introduction ▶

Welcome to *DIY: Guitar*, where we give you all the tools and know-how you need to learn to play guitar in a straight-forward and no-nonsense manner. In that spirit, we don't want to bore you with a lot of mundane, introductory information, so we're going to get right into making music on the instrument.

That being said, there *are* some basic things you should know before you start—like how to tune your guitar—or at least know that you can find in the appendices at the end of this book. There, you'll find a basic glossary of *Guitar Talk*, which explains some of the jargon that guitarists commonly use, and which you'll find on these pages. You'll also find diagrams that identify the key parts of acoustic and electric guitars, a chord reference page, a fretboard diagram that shows you the names of every note on the guitar, and a whole lot of basic music theory, should you wish to learn those fundamentals.

Now, let's get started. First, are you...

New to guitar?

If you're just picking up the guitar for the first time, awesome! You're about to embark on a fun and rewarding journey of learning how to play your favorite songs and even creating your own music.

Or, are you ...

Returning to guitar?

Yeah, we've heard the story countless times. You picked up a guitar years ago and started learning, but then life—college, career, marriage, kids—happened, and now you're finally ready to pick it up again. If so, this book is also for you. You can either start right at the beginning, learning or reviewing basic chords, or skip ahead using the table of contents as a guide, to find the right place to dive in.

Audio and Video 🔊 ▶

Much of the content appearing within the book is demonstrated either through audio examples or video lessons. You can access these files by going to **www.halleonard.com/mylibrary** and inputting the code found on page 1.

Basics

If you're a new or returning player, then it's important to review the basics of posture and body mechanics when playing the guitar.

There are several ways to hold the guitar comfortably. On the left is a typical seated position, and on the right is the standing position. Make sure you practice sitting and standing. Observe the following general guidelines in forming your playing posture:

- Position your body, arms, and legs in such a way that you avoid tension.
- If you feel tension creeping into your playing, you probably need to reassess your position.
- Tilt the neck upwards—never down.
- Keep the body of the guitar as vertical as possible. Avoid slanting the top of the guitar so that you can see better. Balance your weight evenly from left to right. Sit straight (but not rigid).

Left-hand fingers are numbered 1 through 4 (Pianists: Note that the thumb is not number 1.) Place the thumb in back of the neck roughly opposite the 2nd finger. Avoid gripping the neck like a baseball bat with the palm touching the back of the neck.

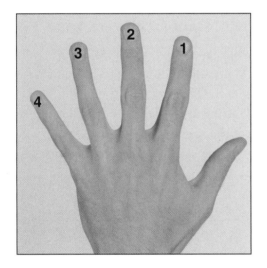 

These photos show the position for holding a pick and the right-hand position in relationship to the strings. Strive for finger efficiency and relaxation in your playing.

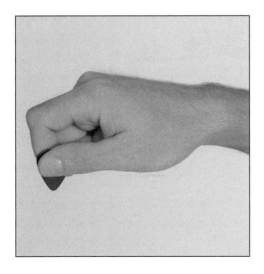 

Tuning

It is *essential* that before you play your first note or chord, you learn how to *tune* your guitar. Whether you're playing an acoustic or an electric guitar, it's tuned the exact same way. The tuning notes, from the lowest (thickest) string to the highest (thinnest) one is: E–A–D–G–B–E. You may also see the strings identified by number, as follows:

6th string = low E (thickest string)
5th string = A
4th string = D
3rd string = G
2nd string = B
1st string = high E (thinnest string)

We've included tuning notes for all six strings in the online audio that accompanies this book. As you compare each tuning note to the matching string on your guitar, you may notice a "beating" sound; the more "out of tune" the two pitches are, the faster the beat. As you twist your tuning peg to either increase (counterclockwise) or release (clockwise) tension on the string, the beating will slow down until the two pitches are in perfect unison, or in tune, with each other.

There will be many times when you might not have access to the online audio but still need to tune your guitar. The best way to do this is to invest in an electronic tuner. You can find small ones that clip onto your guitar's headstock for as little as $10–15, and they're typically quite accurate—even professional guitarists use them.

Once your guitar is tuned, and you've been playing for a little while, you might find that one or two strings have slipped out of tune, usually indicated by strummed chords that don't sound quite right. In that case, you can use the manual "fifth-fret tuning" approach. Here, you'll fret a string at the fifth fret, and the next highest open string should match the pitch. For example, if you fret the 6th (low E) string at the fifth fret, you'll produce an A note, which is the same as the open 5th string. Likewise, the fifth fret of the A string produces a D note, which matches the open 4th string. The only exception is the 3rd string. There, you must move down to the fourth fret to match the open B string right above it.

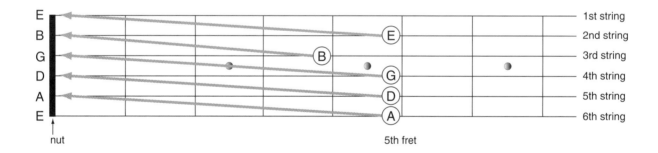

Now that you're all tuned up, let's start playing some guitar!

Chapter 1 ▶
Chord Basics

Unlike the majority of guitar methods through the years, which begin with playing single notes, often in the form of nursery rhyme melodies like "Twinkle, Twinkle, Little Star" or "Mary Had a Little Lamb," this one jumps right into playing chords, common chord progressions, and real songs.

Open Chords

Your first chords are called **open chords**, because they all utilize open strings and are fretted primarily in open position, or the first three frets. You'll sometimes hear these called "cowboy chords," so named for the old-time country artists like Roy Rogers and the singing cowboy himself, Gene Autry, who used open chords extensively in their songs.

The E Minor Chord

Your first chord is E minor, which is written as Em. It's also one of the easiest chords to play on the guitar, requiring just your index finger on the 5th string at the second fret and your middle finger on the 4th string, also at the second fret, with all the remaining strings left to ring open.

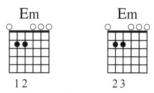

You can—and should—also learn to play this chord using your middle and ring fingers on strings 5 and 4, respectively.

How to Read a Chord Frame
The vertical lines of the frame represent the guitar's six strings, from low to high, moving left to right. The horizontal lines represent the guitar's nut (top, thick line) and then the frets. Open circles above the chord frame indicate those strings should be played open. Black dots on the chord frame depict where your fingers should be placed to play the chord. The numbers below the chord frame tell you which of your fret-hand fingers should be used to fret that note (1=index, 2=middle, 3=ring, 4=pinky). An "X" above the frame means that string should *not* be played in the chord.

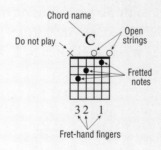

When you strum the Em chord, do all the notes ring clearly? Probably not if that was your first try, but that's OK. Make sure your fret hand's fingers are arched so that each one touches *only* the string it's supposed to touch and then try again.

If you're having trouble getting all the notes to ring out, try a "chord check," where, while holding down all the notes, you play one note at a time starting with the 6th string, to see where the sticking point is.

Now let's try strumming that Em chord again. This time, count, "1–2–3–4," as you play, strumming in a downward motion on each count.

Fig. 1

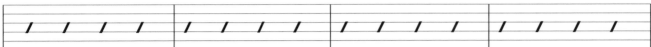

The C Chord

The next open chord you're going to play is C major chord. To play it, place your ring finger on the 5th string at the third fret, your middle finger on the 4th string at the second fret, and your index finger on the 2nd string at the first fret. Strings 3 and 1 should ring open. Unlike the Em chord, however, you do *not* play the 6th string on this one.

Like the Em chord, practice strumming this one in a downward motion, working to ensure all the notes ring clearly. Be sure to start your strumming motion at the 5th string and don't forget to count, "1–2–3–4," while strumming.

Fig. 2

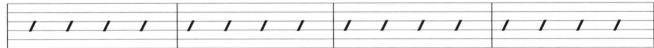

Changing Chords

Now that you know two of the most commonly played chords on the guitar, Em and C, it's time to start switching between them while strumming. In this next exercise, you'll strum the Em chord eight times, then switch to the C chord and strum that eight times, and then repeat (indicated by ‖: :‖ at the beginning and end of a section).

Fig. 3 🔊

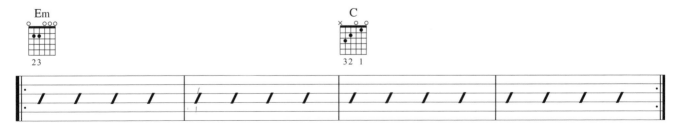

The D Chord

Let's take a look at the open D major chord. This chord has a little bit of a tricky fingering compared to the G and C chords, but its "triangular" shape makes it pretty easy to remember. First, place your index finger on the 3rd string at the second fret, then your middle finger on the 1st string also at the second fret, and your ring finger sort of reaches around and over the middle finger to settle in on the 2nd string at the third fret. As for open strings, you'll play only the open D, or 4th string.

D

Now practice strumming it while counting, "1–2–3–4." Make sure you're not strumming the 6th and 5th strings. Position your pick or thumb, whichever you're using to strum, just above the open D string and strum downward, checking that each note rings clearly.

Fig. 4

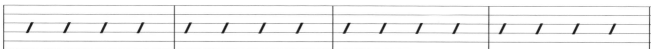

The G Chord

Your next open chord is the G major, which is shown in the chord frame below. To play this G major chord, place your fret-hand's index finger on the 5th string at the second fret, your middle finger on the 6th string at the third fret, and your ring finger on the 1st string at the third fret. Allow the 4th, 3rd, and 2nd strings to all ring open. Once you have all your fingers in place and pushing down on the strings, use your other hand's thumb or a plectrum to strum the strings, from the lowest to the highest.

G

Let's strum that one while counting *1–2–3–4.*

Fig. 5

Like you did with the Em and C chords, you're now going to practice changing between the D and G chords.

Fig. 6

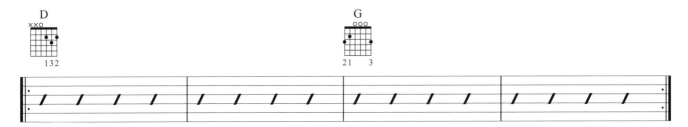

Chord Progressions

You might not realize it, but even though you've learned only four chords, these chords, in various combinations called **chord progressions**, account for *thousands* of songs, including many of the most popular in history.

The reason these four chords go together in so many great songs is that they all belong to the same **key**—in this case, the key of G. You'll learn more about musical keys later in this book, but for now, just know that you're playing in the key of G, and that these four particular chords—G, C, D, Em—all belong to that key.

Let's practice playing these four chords in various progressions, with a focus on getting comfortable making the changes between chords as smoothly as you can.

Fig. 7

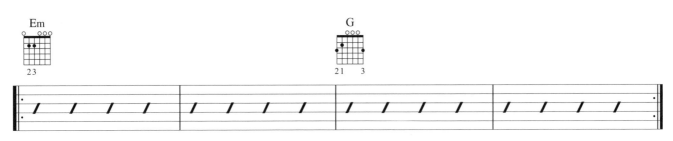

Fig. 8

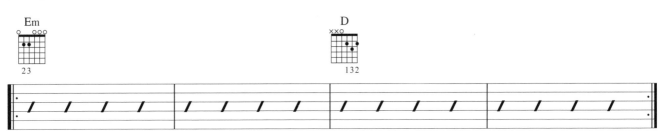

Fig. 9

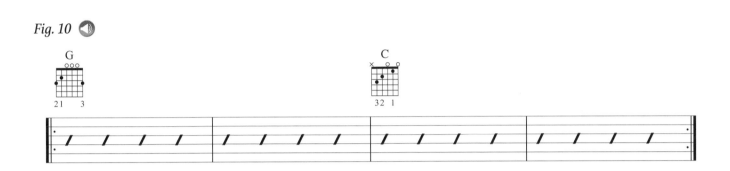

Fig. 10

Jam Time

Now it's time to place those chord progressions in the context of actual songs. In this next section, you'll play various combinations of the G, C, D, and Em chords while at the same time playing key parts of a number of classic songs.

To make it a little more fun, we're going to present these song snippets with the lyrics, to help you know exactly what you're playing—and so you can sing along, if you'd like. For these songs, you'll notice we've removed the staff and instead just placed the chord symbols above the lyrics. Simply change chords whenever you come to a new symbol in the song. As for strumming, you can continue using the basic four down strums, or feel free to get creative and make up your own.

"SPACE ODDITY"
Words and Music by David Bowie

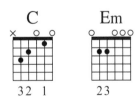

C   **Em** **C**   **Em**
Ground Control to Major Tom, Ground Control to Major Tom.

"YELLOW SUBMARINE"
Words and Music by John Lennon and Paul McCartney

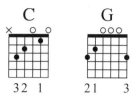

C	G		C
We all live in a yellow submarine, yellow submarine, yellow submarine.

"ELEANOR RIGBY"
Words and Music by John Lennon and Paul McCartney

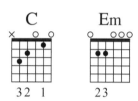

Intro

C   Em   C   Em

Ah, look at all the lonely people! Ah, look at all the lonely people!

Verse

Em   C   Em

Eleanor Rigby picks up the rice in the church where a wedding has been, lives in a dream.

C   Em

Waits at the window, wearing a face that she keeps in a jar by the door. Who is it for?

Chorus

Em   C   Em

All the lonely people, where do they all come from?

C   Em

All the lonely people, where do they all belong?

"RING OF FIRE"
Words and Music by Merle Kilgore and June Carter

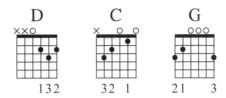

Chorus

D   C   G   D   C   G

I fell into a burning ring of fire. I went down, down, down, and the flames went higher.

                   D   G   D   G

And it burns, burns, burns, the ring of fire, the ring of fire.

"PERFECT"
Words and Music by Ed Sheeran

(If you play along to Ed Sheeran's recording, you'll need to place a **capo** at the first fret; see the appendix in the back if you don't know what a capo is.)

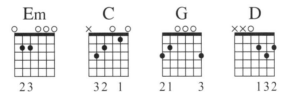

Chorus

     Em C   G   D   Em

Baby, I'm dancing in the dark with you between my arms.

C   G   D   Em

Barefoot on the grass, listening to our favorite song.

       C   G   D   Em

When you said you looked a mess, I whispered underneath my breath.

     C   G   D   G

But you heard it, darling, you look perfect tonight.

"WAGON WHEEL"

Words and Music by Bob Dylan and Ketch Secor

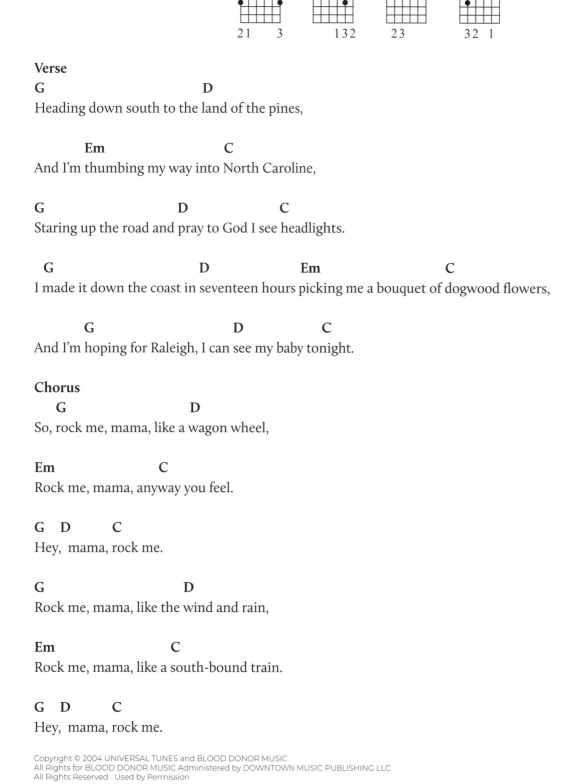

Verse

G   D

Heading down south to the land of the pines,

      Em   C

And I'm thumbing my way into North Caroline,

G   D   C

Staring up the road and pray to God I see headlights.

 G   D   Em   C

I made it down the coast in seventeen hours picking me a bouquet of dogwood flowers,

     G   D   C

And I'm hoping for Raleigh, I can see my baby tonight.

Chorus

  G   D

So, rock me, mama, like a wagon wheel,

Em   C

Rock me, mama, anyway you feel.

G D   C

Hey, mama, rock me.

G   D

Rock me, mama, like the wind and rain,

Em   C

Rock me, mama, like a south-bound train.

G D   C

Hey, mama, rock me.

"I'M YOURS"

Words and Music by Jason Mraz

(If you play along to Jason Mraz's recording, you'll need to place a capo at the first fret.)

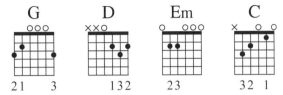

Verse

    G

Well, you done, done me in, you bet I felt it.

  D

I tried to be chill, but you're so hot that I melted.

   Em   C

I fell right through the cracks, now I'm trying to get back.

      G

Before the cool done run out, I'll be giving it my bestest,

  D

And nothing's gonna stop me but divine intervention,

   Em   C

I reckon it's again my turn to win some or learn some.

Chorus

   G   D   Em

But I won't hesitate no more, no more.

     C

It cannot wait, I'm yours.

This acoustic ballad by 1990s punk rockers Green Day was a massive crossover hit, appealing to audiences young and old. It contains just G, C, D, and Em chords, and although the original recording has a somewhat intricate strumming rhythm, you can play this using just down and up strums throughout. That being said, try to come up with your own strumming patterns as you play through the song. Trust us, you really can't go wrong, so be adventurous.

"GOOD RIDDANCE (TIME OF YOUR LIFE)"

Words by Billie Joe
Music by Green Day

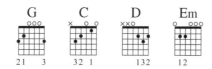

Intro
Very fast

‖: G | | C | D :‖

Verse 1

G   C   D
   Another turnin' point, a fork stuck in the road.

G   C   D
   Time grabs you by the wrist, directs you where to go.

Em   D   C   G
   So make the best of this test, and don't ask why.

Em   D   C   G
   It's not a question but a lesson learned in time.

Chorus

     Em   G   Em   G
It's something unpredictable, but in the end is right.

     Em   D   G
I hope you had the time of your life.

Repeat Intro (2 times)

Verse 2

G   C   D
   So take the photographs and still frames in your mind.

G   C   D
   Hang it on a shelf in good health and good time.

Em   D   C   G
   Tattoos of memories and dead skin on trial.

Em   D   C   G
   For what it's worth, it was worth all the while.

Repeat Chorus

Interlude

Play 4 times

‖: G | | C | D :‖

Play 2 times

‖: Em | D | C | G :‖

Repeat Chorus

Repeat Intro (2 times)

Repeat Chorus

Outro

‖: G | | C | D :‖ G | ‖

Chapter 2
New Chords and Strums

In this chapter, we're going to continue working on chords—learning four new ones, playing in a new key, combining these new chords with ones you've already learned, and trying out a popular strumming pattern.

Learning New Chords

The A Minor Chord
Your next chord is A minor (Am), which also is a member of the key of G, like the four chords you learned already. To play Am, place your middle finger on the 4th string at the second fret, your ring finger on the 3rd string, also at the second fret, your index finger on the 2nd string at the first fret, and leave the 5th and 1st strings to ring open. Do not play the 6th string.

Am

2 3 1

Like you did last chapter, let's practice the Am chord using down strums, counting, "1–2–3–4," as you play.

Fig. 11

 Am

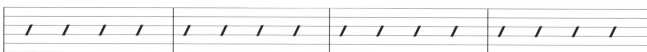

Now let's put that Am chord to work in a basic progression with a C chord. But first, let's take a closer look at the two chord shapes.

 Am   C

2 3 1   3 2   1

Note that both your index and your middle finger are in the same location for both chords; only your ring finger placement changes. Because of that, when you make the change from Am to C or from C to Am, only your ring finger should move. There is no need to pick up your index and middle fingers.

As you play through the exercise below, focus on keeping those two fingers in place when switching chords.

Fig. 12

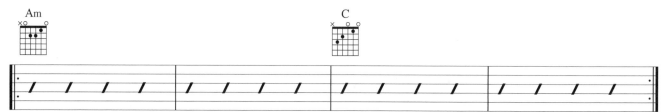

Am   C

When two chords share notes, we call those notes **common tones**, and these common tones often—but not always—come with a common fingering. Watch for common fingerings whenever you play chords, to help make the changes much easier. In time and with experience, it will all become second nature.

The A Major Chord

The next essential open chord is A major (A). There are actually several ways that guitarists play the A major chord, but the two fingerings presented here are probably the most popular. Based on what your fingers have already learned, it's probably easiest to start by fingering an Am chord, then removing your index finger from the 2nd string at the first fret and instead just drop your pinky finger down on the 2nd string at the second fret, leaving the 5th and 1st strings open, and not playing the 6th string.

Alternatively, since you will *rarely* change from Am to A in a real song, the common fingering it offers isn't very important. Many guitarists instead prefer to use their index finger on the 4th string, middle finger on the 3rd string, and ring finger on the 2nd string—all at the second fret.

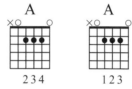

Use the exercise below to try both fingerings and, for now, use the one that feels most comfortable to you.

Fig. 13 🔊

Hopefully you found a fingering that feels best to you, but context is important, too. One of the most common chord changes you'll make involving the A major chord is to go from A to D. Try that progression below, again using both A major chord fingerings to see if one is easier for you than the other when playing it in a more musical setting.

Fig. 14 🔊

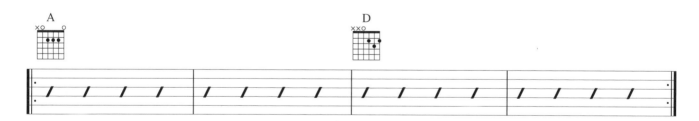

The E Major Chord

Next up is the E major chord. To play this one, first finger the Em chord you've already learned, then just place your index finger on the 3rd string at the first fret, leaving the 6th, 2nd, and 1st strings all open to ring.

Down-Up Strumming

So far, you've only used down strums for all the chord exercises in this book, counting, "1–2–3–4," repeatedly as you strummed. It would be a bit surprising if you're not a little bored with that by now, so let's double it up! For the rest of this chapter, you should still count, "1–2–3–4," but now, you're going to add the word "and" between each number, counting, "1–and–2–and–3–and–4–and," and you're going to use an **up strum** each time you say "and." So you'll be strumming in a "down-up, down-up, down-up, down-up" pattern. In the graphic below, the small symbol above the staff that looks sort of like a table ⊓ indicates a down strum, whereas the "V" shape ⋁ indicates an up strum.

Strum Pattern 1

Because you play all six strings with the E major chord, it's a good one to try the **down-up** strum, so give it a go. Remember to count, "1–and–2–and–3–and–4–and," as you strum.

Fig. 15

Count: 1 and 2 and 3 and 4 and *sim.*

Like the A–D progression you learned earlier in this chapter, the E–A progression is also very common in pop and rock music. If you can, use the down-up strum pattern for the following exercise, but feel free to start with just down strums if you need to at first.

Fig. 16

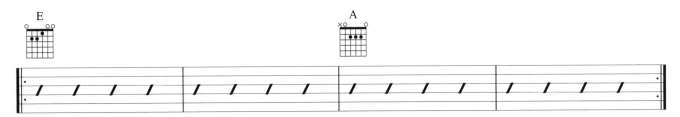

The D Minor Chord

The final chord you'll learn this chapter is the D minor (Dm) chord. To play this chord, place your middle finger on the 3rd string at the second fret, your ring finger on the 2nd string at the third fret, and your index finger on the 1st string at the first fret. Let the 4th string ring open, but do not play the 5th or 6th strings.

Let's try strumming the Dm chord. If you want to try down-up strum pattern, by all means, do so. But since this chord uses only four strings, it might be a little more challenging.

Fig. 17

The next exercise switches between Am and Dm chords.

Fig. 18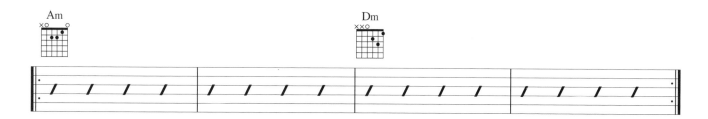

Playing in Different Keys

Unlike the chords in Chapter 1, the four new ones you've learned in this chapter don't all belong to a single key. However, two of them—A and E—go with the D major chord to form the trio of major chords that belong to the key of A major. The first progression you'll play in the next section, A–D–A–E, is one of the most common in the key of A.

Chord Progressions

Now put this chapter's four new chords to work, along with the four you already learned, in popular chord progressions.

Fig. 19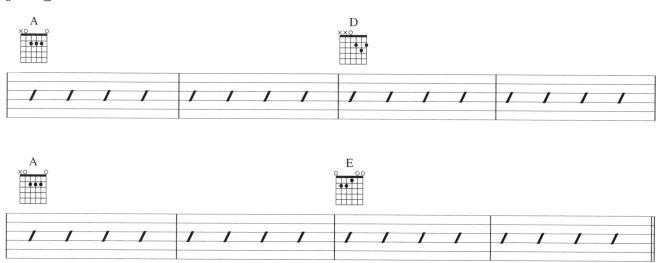

Fig. 20

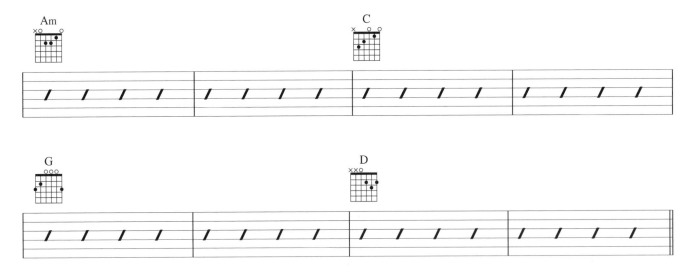

Fig. 21

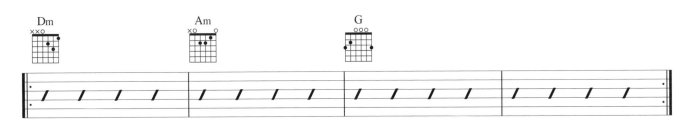

Fig. 22

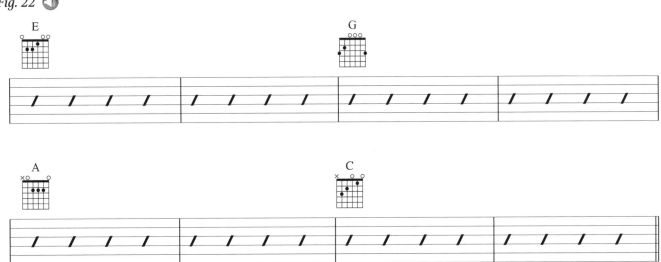

Fig. 23

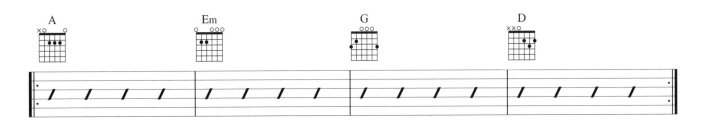

Strum Patterns

In Strum Pattern 1, you split each beat in half, which means you strummed eight times—down–up–down–up–down–up–down–up—in each count of four (1–and–2–and–3–and–4–and). In Strum Pattern 2, you'll alternate whole and split beats so that you're strumming down–down–up–down–down–up while counting, "1–2–and–3–4–and." For Strum Pattern 3, use just a down strum on beats 1 and 2, then switch to down–up–down–up for beats 3 and 4 (down–down–down–up–down–up) while counting, "1–2–3–and–4–and."

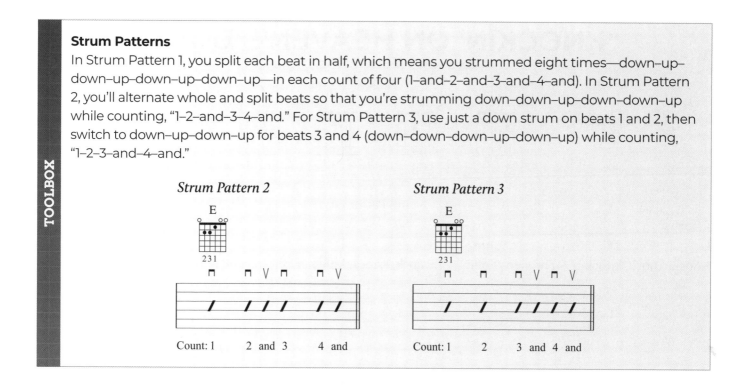

Jam Time

Let's play some songs that feature various combinations of the eight chords you've learned so far. We've included a recommended strum pattern for each, but feel free to experiment or even make up your own.

"THREE LITTLE BIRDS"
Words and Music by Bob Marley

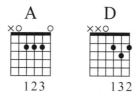

Strum Pattern #2

Chorus

    A
Don't worry about a thing,
    D   **A**
'Cos ev' ry little thing gonna be alright.

Singin' don't worry about a thing,
    D
'Cos ev' ry little thing gonna be alright!

"KNOCKIN' ON HEAVEN'S DOOR"

Words and Music by Bob Dylan

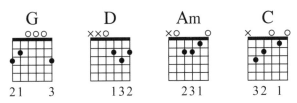

Strum Pattern #2

Chorus

G	D	Am

Knock, knock, knockin' on heaven's door.

G	D	C

Knock, knock, knockin' on heaven's door.

"BYE BYE LOVE"

Words and Music by Felice Bryant and Boudleaux Bryant

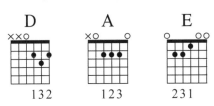

Strum Pattern #2 or #3

Chorus

D   A
Bye bye   love,
D   A
Bye bye   happiness.
D   A
     Hello   loneliness.
           E   A
I think I'm-a gonna cry.

"CLOCKS"

Words and Music by Guy Berryman, Jon Buckland, Will Champion and Chris Martin

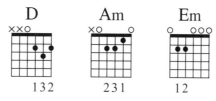

Strum Pattern #3

Verse

D   Am
The lights go out and I can't be saved,
                 Em
Tides that I tried to swim against
D   Am
Have brought me down up on my knees,

                 Em
Oh,   I   beg,   I   beg and plead,

         D   Am
Singing: come out   of   things unsaid,
                 Em
Shoot   an   apple off my head.
        D   Am
And a   trouble   that   can't be named
                Em
A tiger's   waiting   to be tamed.   Singing

Chorus

D | Am | Am | Em
       You | | are. | |
D | Am | Am | Em
       You | | are. | |

To close out Chapter 2, you're going to play the Creedence Clearwater Revival classic "Fortunate Son," which contains the A, G, D, and E chords. You're also going to see a new element called **tablature**, or **tab**, at the start of the song and in the middle. Tab is a form of music notation used for various stringed instruments, most commonly guitar. If you don't know how to read tab, turn the page and take a look at the start of Chapter 3 for a full explanation.

"Fortunate Son" appears on the next page to allow for easier reading.

"FORTUNATE SON"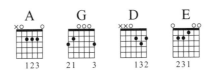

Words and Music by John Fogerty

Intro (Drums only 2 measures)
Moderately

```
    5              3              2              0
T|--6------------|--4----------|--2----------|--2----------------|
A|              |            |            |              3--0  |
B|              |            |            |                    |
```

Verse 1

A   G
Some folks are born, made to wave the flag,

D   A
Ooh, their red, white and blue.

                     G
And when the band plays, "Hail to the Chief,"

D   A
Ooh, they point the cannon at you, Lord.

Chorus 1

A   E
But it ain't me, it ain't me,

D   A
I ain't no senator's son, son.

        E
It ain't me, it ain't me,

D   A
I ain't no fortunate one, no.

Verse 2

A   G
Some folks are born, silver spoon in hand,

D   A
Lord, don't they help themselves, y'all?

                G
But when the taxman come to the door,

D   A
Lord, the house look like a rummage sale, yeah, now.

Chorus 2

   A   E

      Well, it ain't me,   it ain't me,

   D   A

      I ain't no millionaire's son, no, no.

                   E

      It ain't me,   it ain't me,

   D   A

      I ain't no fortunate one, no.

Interlude

Verse 3

   A   G

      Some folks inherit star-spangled eyes.

   D   A

      Ooh, they send you down to war, y'all.

                     G

      And when you ask 'em, "How much should we give?"

   D   A

      Ooh, they only answer, "More, more, more," y'all.

Chorus 3

  A   E   D   A

    It ain't me,   it ain't me,   I ain't no military son, son.

  A   E   D   A   ***Repeat and fade***

‖:   It ain't me, | it ain't me, | I ain't no fortunate| one, no.   :‖

Chapter 3 ▶

Single Notes and Tab

In this chapter, you're going to begin playing single-note melodies, be introduced to the tab form of music notation, and learn a couple of new chords.

Single Notes

Although guitarists spend most of their time playing chords—which is the main reason this book starts with them—you'll also play a lot of single-note melodies and phrases along the way. Before we can show you how to play single-note lines, though, you first need to learn how to read the tab notation used to teach them.

Introduction to Tab Notation

Starting in this next section, we're going to use the guitar notation system known as tablature, or tab, for short. Tab notation uses six horizontal lines representing the six strings of a guitar as the staff. The top line represents the high E, or 1st, string. The line below that represents the B, or 2nd, string, and so forth. The numbers that appear on the lines tell you at which fret you should place your finger on that particular string, with a "0" indicating that the string should be played open. Chords are represented with the numbers in a vertical column, meaning all the chord's notes should be played at the same time (e.g., strummed).

In the example below, the first tab number "0" on the bottom line indicates that you should play the 6th string open. The "2" on the next line up indicates that you should next play the 5th string with a finger (use your middle finger) at the second fret. When the notes are stacked in tab, it means they are played together, so place your index finger on the 3rd string at the first fret and your ring finger on the 4th string at the second fret and strum or pick just those two strings. The final set of tab notes represents a chord; can you identify it? Yep, it's an E major chord.

Reading Tab Notation 🔊

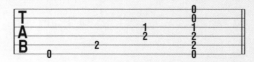

To begin your single-note odyssey, let's start with a *very* basic exercise in which you'll simply play all six open strings. Whether you're using a pick or your thumb to pluck these notes, the idea here is to introduce you to the idea of playing just one note at a time.

Fig. 24 🔊

And now let's try a similar exercise but with fretted notes added to it. Use your ring finger for all the notes at the third fret and your middle finger for all the notes at the second fret.

Fig. 25 🔊

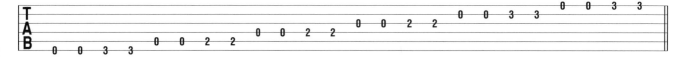

You probably don't know it, but you just played your first scale! Yep, that exercise was made up of the notes from the **E minor pentatonic scale**. We'll go over this scale in greater detail in Chapter 9, when you begin learning how to play licks and solos. For now, though, it serves as a great single-string exercise. So let's play it again using the same fingers, only this time, backwards.

Fig. 26 🔊

This next exercise is also a scale—the **G major scale**, as played on strings 3–1, and which you'll learn in more complete form in Chapter 11. You don't need to know the names of the notes right now, but if you're curious, you can compare them to the fretboard diagram in the appendix of the book.

Fig. 27 🔊

Jam Time

Now let's try playing some famous melodies using single notes on the top three strings. For these, assign your index finger to all first-fret notes, middle to all second-fret notes, and ring finger to all third-fret notes.

Here's arguably the most popular song the world has ever known, "Happy Birthday," arranged for you to practice playing single notes.

"HAPPY BIRTHDAY TO YOU"
Words and Music by Mildred J. Hill and Patty S. Hill

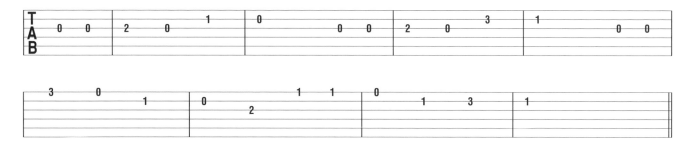

"STAR WARS (MAIN THEME)"
(from *Star Wars: A New Hope*)
Music by John Williams

SPONGEBOB SQUAREPANTS THEME SONG
(from *Spongebob Squarepants*)
Words and Music by Mark Harrison, Blaise Smith, Steve Hillenburg and Derek Drymon

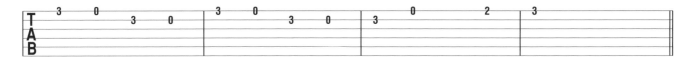

"DUELIN' BANJOS"
By Arthur Smith

THE ANDY GRIFFITH SHOW THEME
(THE FISHIN' HOLE)
By Earle Hagen and Herbert Spencer

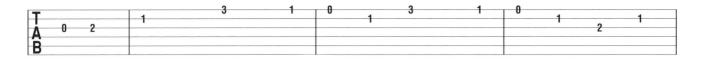

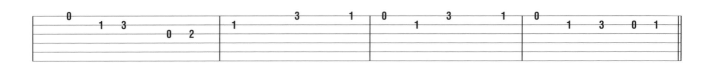

New Chords

Great work on those single notes! Now let's take a look at a couple of new chords and play a few progressions using them.

The B Minor Chord

First up is the B minor (Bm) chord, which uses all four of your fret hand's fingers. You can think of this one as being nearly the same as the Am chord shape, but moved up two frets and played with different fingers. Here, place your index finger on the 5th string at the second fret, your ring finger on the 4th string at the fourth fret, your pinky finger on the 3rd string also at the fourth fret, and your middle finger on the 2nd string at the third fret. Neither the 6th nor the 1st strings are played in this version of the chord.

Let's try strumming the Bm chord. Start with down strums only, to make it easier to avoid striking the 6th and 1st strings. Once you're comfortable, try the down-up strum pattern.

Fig. 28

Now let's try switching between Bm and D chords. This might be the toughest chord change you've had to make so far, so take your time and practice at a slow enough pace that you can make the change while counting, "1–2–3–4," without a pause.

Fig. 29

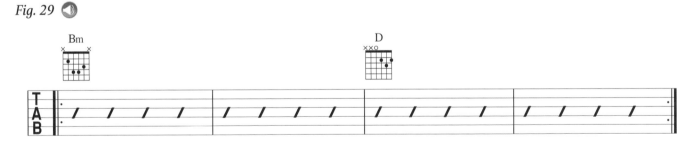

The F Major Chord

So far, all of the chords you've learned have required only one string per finger. The F major chord, though, presents a new challenge: holding down *two* strings with a single finger at the same time! To play F major, place your ring finger on the 4th string at the third fret, your middle finger on the 3rd string at the second fret, and your index finger on *both* the 2nd and 1st strings, at the first fret. To do so, first place it on just the 2nd string at the first fret, then "flatten" it so that it also presses down the 1st string.

The technique of holding down multiple strings with a single finger is called the **barre** technique. Perhaps you've heard of **barre chords**. It's a term that strikes fear into less-motivated beginner guitarists, but we're certain that you'll see it as a challenge to meet and overcome. No doubt, this is a tricky devil, and it's most likely going to take a lot more practice than what you've needed with other chords so far, but mastering the barre technique is essential to becoming a complete guitarist. Once you're able to consistently generate a clean sound, try strumming the F chord in all three strum patterns.

Fig. 30

Now try changing from F to Dm. Note that if you are able to properly hold down the barre in the F chord, you only need to lift your ring finger from the third fret on the 4th string and place it at the third fret of the 2nd string to make the change, leaving your middle and index fingers in place. If it's too difficult to hold the barre during the Dm chord, though, feel free to play that chord the normal way.

Fig. 31

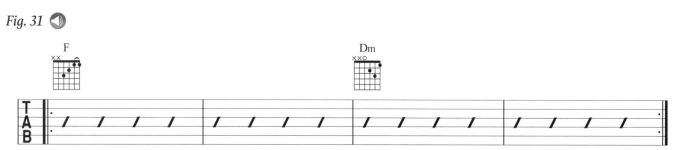

Chord Progressions

The two new chords you learned, Bm and F, each belong to several keys, but we're going to focus on just one key, or chord family, for each.

The Key of D

You've previously learned the D, G, and A major chords as well as Em. If you add the Bm to that group, you've got five chords that all belong to the key of D major, which means you can play a multitude of chord progressions using various combinations of those chords, as heard in myriad classic hits. Let's take a look at a couple of the most popular progressions in the key of D.

This first one uses the D, A, Bm, and G chords, in that order.

Fig. 32

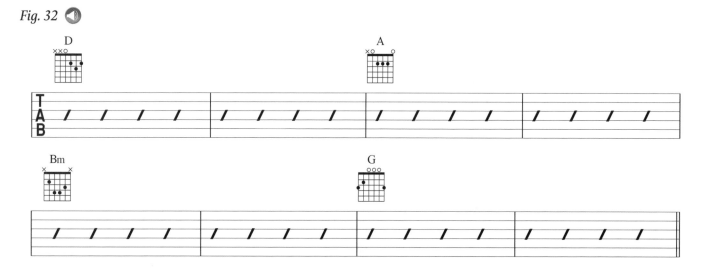

This next progression uses all five of the chords you've learned from the key of D.

Fig. 33

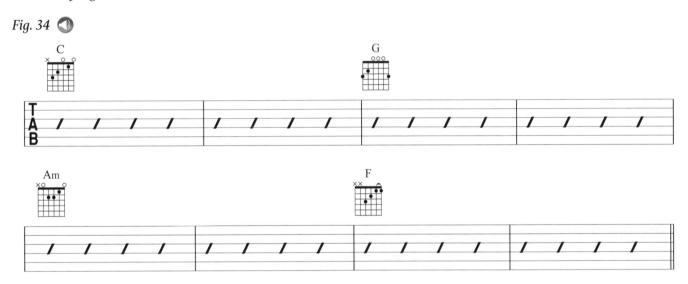

The Key of C

So far, you've learned the chords C, Dm, Em, G, and Am, which all fit into the key of C. Now you can add the F major chord to that list.

This first progression uses the C, G, Am, and F chords.

Fig. 34

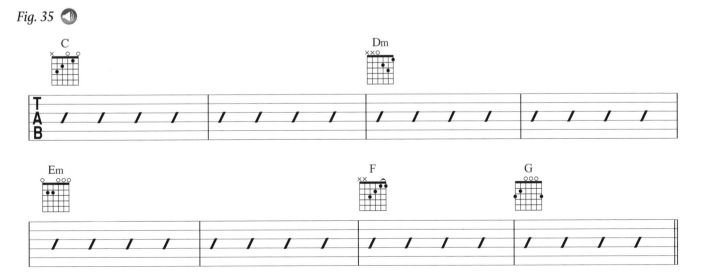

This next progression uses the first five chords from the key of C, in order. For added practice on any of these progressions, repeat the progression as often as it takes to achieve smooth chord changes.

Fig. 35

Jam Time

Nice work on the new chords! Now let's play a couple of tunes to put them to work.

"LET IT BE"

Words and Music by John Lennon and Paul McCartney

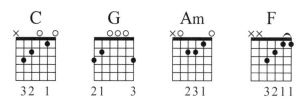

Verse

      C   G

When I find myself in times of trouble,

Am   **F**

Mother Mary comes to me,

C   **G**   **F**

Speaking words of wisdom, let it be.

     C   **G**   **Am**   **F**

And in my hour of darkness she is standing right in front of me,

C   **G**   **F**   **C**

Speaking words of wisdom, let it be.

Chorus

      Am   **G**   **F**   **C**

Let it be, let it be, let it be, let it be.

                G   **F**   **C**

Whisper words of wisdom, let it be.

"JUST LIKE HEAVEN"

Words by Robert Smith

Music by Robert Smith, Laurence Tolhurst, Simon Gallup, Paul S. Thompson and Boris Williams

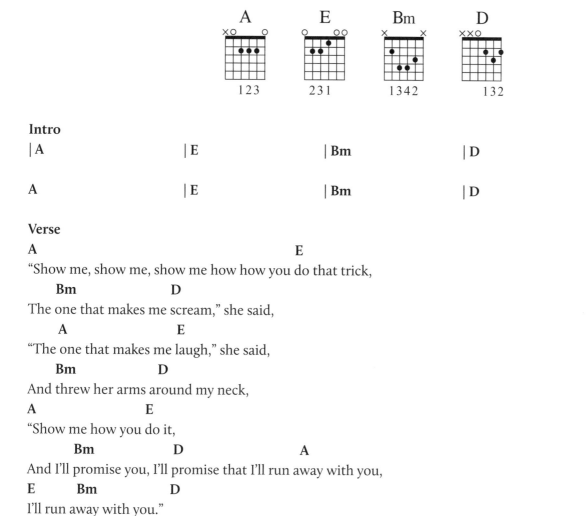

Intro

| A | E | Bm | D |

A | E | Bm | D

Verse

A   E
"Show me, show me, show me how how you do that trick,
      Bm   **D**
The one that makes me scream," she said,
       A   **E**
"The one that makes me laugh," she said,
      Bm   **D**
And threw her arms around my neck,
A   **E**
"Show me how you do it,
      Bm   **D**   **A**
And I'll promise you, I'll promise that I'll run away with you,
E   **Bm**   **D**
I'll run away with you."

To close out Chapter 3, you're going to rock out on one of the most popular party sing-alongs of all time: "Brown Eyed Girl" by Van Morrison. Although it doesn't contain either of the new chords you learned this chapter, it does contain one you haven't learned yet: D7. Look at the chord frame to see how to play it. If you feel you aren't up for the challenge, though, you can just substitute a regular D major chord for it, but the D7 really does give the song that extra character.

You'll also see a single-note, simplified version of the classic intro. Given your excellent work on single notes this chapter, this should pose no problems for you.

> "Brown Eyed Girl" appears on the next page to allow for easier reading.

"BROWN EYED GIRL"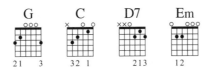

Words and Music by Van Morrison

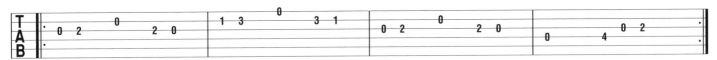

Intro
Moderately fast

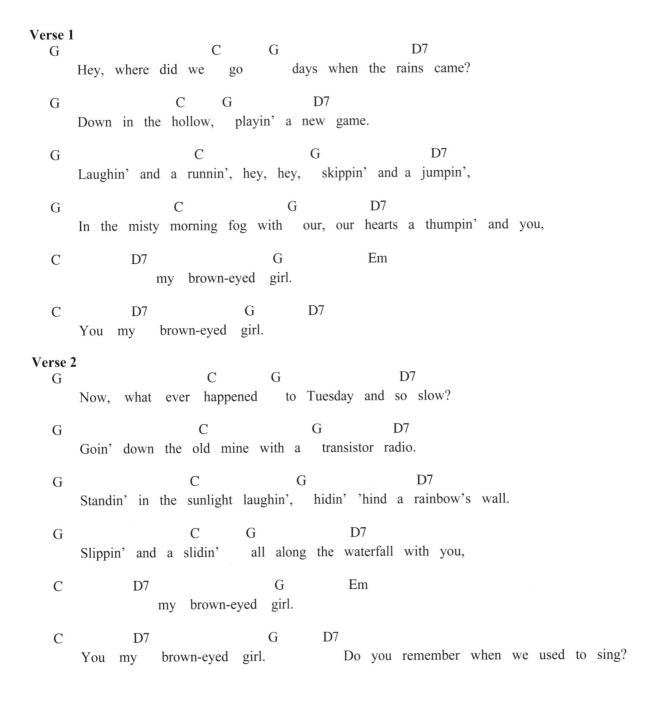

Verse 1

G   C   G   D7
Hey, where did we   go   days when the rains came?

G   C   G   D7
Down in the hollow,   playin' a new game.

G   C   G   D7
Laughin' and a runnin', hey, hey,   skippin' and a jumpin',

G   C   G   D7
In the misty morning fog with   our, our hearts a thumpin' and you,

C   D7   G   Em
      my   brown-eyed   girl.

C   D7   G   D7
You   my   brown-eyed   girl.

Verse 2

G   C   G   D7
Now, what ever happened   to Tuesday and so slow?

G   C   G   D7
Goin' down the old mine with a   transistor radio.

G   C   G   D7
Standin' in the sunlight laughin',   hidin' 'hind a rainbow's wall.

G   C   G   D7
Slippin' and a slidin'   all along the waterfall with you,

C   D7   G   Em
      my   brown-eyed   girl.

C   D7   G   D7
You   my   brown-eyed   girl.   Do you remember when we used to sing?

Chorus

```
G               C           G               D7
  Sha,  la,  la,  la,  la,  la,  la,  la,  la,  la,  la,  te,  da.


G               C           G               D7
  Sha,  la,  la,  la,  la,  la,  la,  la,  la,  la,  la,  te,  da.   La, te, da.


G            |              |   N.C.     |                ‖


```

Interlude

```
G         | C          | G           | D7           ‖
```

Verse 3

```
G               C           G               D7
  So  hard  to  find  my  way    now  that  I'm  all  on  my  own.


G                    C         G        D7
  I  saw  you  just  the  other  day,    my,  how  you  have  grown.


G                      C              G                    D7
Cast  my  mem'ry  back  there,  Lord.      Sometimes,  I'm  overcome  thinkin'  'bout  it.


G                    C            G          D7
  Makin'  love  in  the  green  grass    behind  the  stadium  with  you,


C         D7                 G              Em
            my   brown-eyed   girl.


C         D7                 G        D7
  You  my   brown-eyed   girl.        Do  you  remember  when  we  used  to  sing?
```

Outro-Chorus *(Repeat and Fade)*

```
G               C           G               D7
  Sha,  la,  la,  la,  la,  la,  la,  la,  la,  la,  la,  te,  da.
```

Chapter 4 ▶
Reading Rhythms

In this chapter, you'll learn how to read and play basic rhythms, a fine selection of classic guitar riffs, and an alternative to strumming chords.

Rhythm Tab

Hopefully, you've been counting, "1–2–3–4," while playing all of the chord and scale exercises so far, as well as the "and" when using the down-up Strum Pattern 1. The reason you were asked to do so was to begin to develop a sense of **rhythm**, or time. At its core, music is made up of melody, harmony, and rhythm; that is, which notes to play and when to play them.

But just placing tab numbers close together or far apart—as you've seen so far—is not a very accurate way of conveying the rhythm of a chord progression or melodic phrase. By now, you should be getting comfortable enough with the physical parts of playing chords and single notes that you can start learning actual rhythms.

To begin, take a look at the example below.

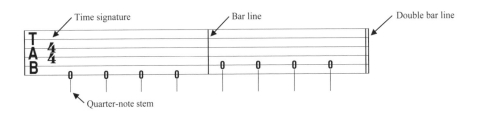

This figure is set in **rhythm tab**, which adds time values to the tab numbers. It comprises two **measures**, which are defined by vertical **bar lines** that dissect the tab staff into equal sections. (No doubt you've already observed this in the previous pages of the book.) You'll see that each measure (also called a bar) of this example contains four notes, with each note receiving one beat. Because each note is one of four notes in the measure, it's called a **quarter note**, and the way quarter notes are shown in rhythm tab is to add a vertical line, called a **stem**, attached to the tab number. And finally, the stacked numerals on the left are called a **time signature**, which tells you how many beats are in each measure (top number) and what kind of note is counted as a beat (bottom number). So in 4/4 time (say "four-four"), there are four beats in each measure, and a quarter note is counted as one beat.

Here's a very simple single-note example set in a quarter-note rhythm in 4/4 time, so you play one note per beat. Set a metronome to about 48 beats per minute (bpm), tap your foot in time to it, and play a note on each downbeat, or foot tap, counting, "1–2–3–4," as you go. Use your index finger at the first fret, middle finger at the second fret, and ring finger at the third fret. Continue the pattern onto strings 2 and 1 for extra practice.

Fig. 36 🔊

Riffs

One of the most common types of single-note lines you'll play is a **riff**, which is just a repeated melodic line. On guitar, they are often composed of single notes that are typically—though by no means exclusively—played on the lowest three strings (strings 6–4).

Let's try a couple of quarter-note riffs, making sure to count, "1–2–3–4," assigning one number to each beat or foot tap (i.e., count "1" on beat 1, "2" on beat 2, and so on).

This first one, which is in the style of Led Zeppelin's "Dazed and Confused," is similar to the previous exercise, only played backward.

Fig. 37

Here's a very popular quarter-note blues riff. Use your index finger for the second-fret notes, your ring finger for the fourth-fret notes, and your pinky for the fifth-fret note.

Fig. 38

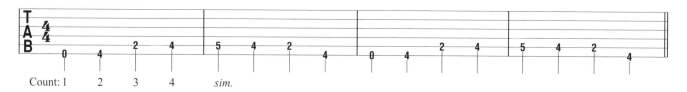

Eighth Notes

Remember the earlier chord and riff exercises for which you had to count, "1-and-2-and-3-and-4-and?" In those instances, you were playing two notes in the space of one beat, and since a quarter note gets the beat, you were playing half of a quarter note, which, if you'll recall from fourth-grade math class, is one eighth (1/8), or an **eighth note**. In other words, one eighth note equals half a beat, and two eighth notes equal one beat.

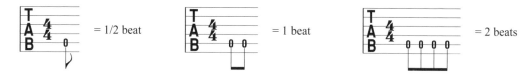

So, as shown above, a single eighth note looks like a quarter note, but with a little "flag" attached to the stem. A pair of eighth notes is notated using a horizontal "beam" connecting the stems. And finally, any four consecutive eighth notes occurring either on beats 1-2 or 3-4 will be notated with a horizontal beam connecting all four stems.

Let's try some simple eighth-note riffs. Tap your foot in a quarter-note rhythm (1-2-3-4), and count, "1-and-2-and-3-and-4-and" for the eighth notes.

Fig. 39

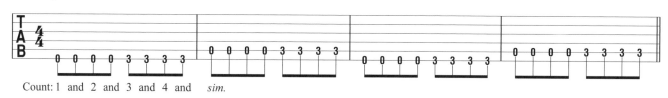

Here's the same basic riff, but this time it mixes quarter notes and eighth notes.

Fig. 40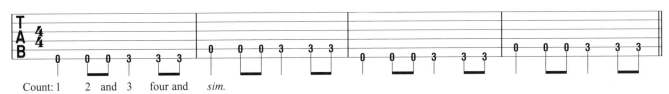

Alternate Picking

When you learned Strum Pattern 1, you performed both down strums and up strums. You can apply the same technique to playing single-note riffs and melodies, particularly those containing eighth notes. Let's revisit that last riff you played (Fig. 39), but this time, as you count the rhythm, you'll use a downstroke on every downbeat (1–2–3–4) and an upstroke on every upbeat ("and"); this technique is called **alternate picking**.

Alternate Picking and Changing Strings

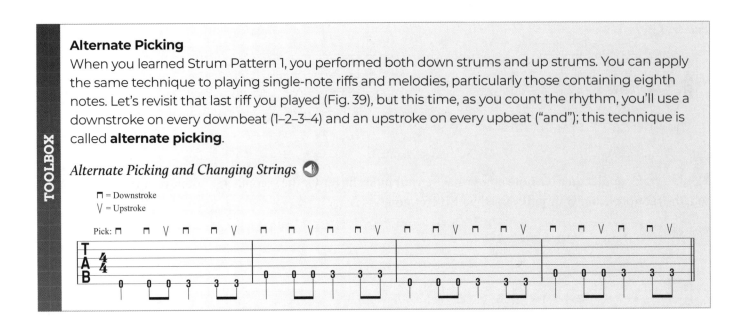

Let's try one more permutation of the riff, again combining quarter notes and eighth notes, and this time use the alternate picking technique on the eighth notes.

Fig. 41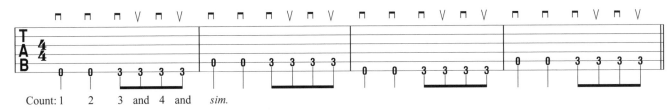

OK, here's another classic rock–style riff on the bottom two strings that you can use to practice not only alternate picking but also various fret-finger combinations. As you can see, the only fretted notes are at the third and fourth frets. Most seasoned guitarists would use the middle and ring fingers on frets 3 and 4, respectively, for this riff. Start with that combination, but then for added practice, try using your index and middle fingers, or even your ring and pinky fingers.

Fig. 42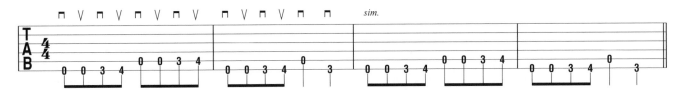

Next up is an oldies-style rock 'n' roll riff composed entirely of eighth notes. Be sure to use alternate picking on this one.

Fig. 43 🔊

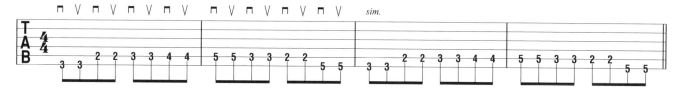

And finally, a heavy metal riff that also uses all four fingers, only fretted notes, and alternate picking.

Fig. 44 🔊

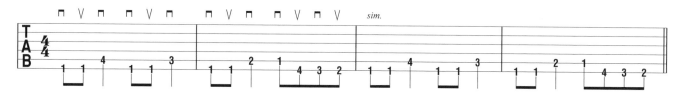

Jam Time

Enough with the exercises—let's play some real riffs. Remember to tap your foot on each quarter-note beat and use your counting to keep good time and rhythm.

"PETER GUNN THEME"
by Henry Mancini

Use one finger per fret on this classic riff; that is, your index finger on the second fret, middle on the third, ring on the fourth, and pinky on the fifth.

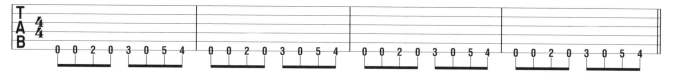

"BEDS ARE BURNING"
Words and Music by Robert Hirst, James Moginie and Peter Garrett

Similar to the "Peter Gunn Theme" above, this '80s hit from the Australian rock band Midnight Oil also features fretted notes alternating with the open low E string. But this one requires you to shift your hand position. It's best to play the lower note of each pair of fretted notes with your index finger. Follow the fingering instructions in the figure.

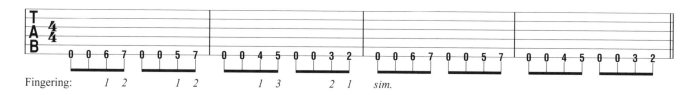

"LADY MADONNA"
Words and Music by John Lennon and Paul McCartney

Use your index, middle, and ring fingers for the notes at the second, third, and fourth frets, respectively. See that circled "2" at the end with a stem? A circled tab number with a stem indicates a **half note**, which is held for two full beats (or, half a measure in 4/4 time).

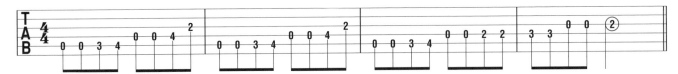

"COME AS YOU ARE"
Words and Music by Kurt Cobain

This grunge hit from Nirvana has both quarter notes and eighth notes, so watch your counting.

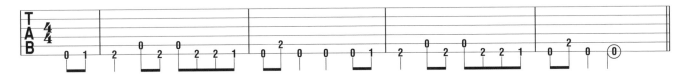

"CRAZY TRAIN"
Words and Music by Ozzy Osbourne, Randy Rhoads and Bob Daisley

All aboard! One of the most famous rock guitar riffs in history, this one is a little tricky with the rapid alternations between the 6th and 5th strings. Place your fret hand's index finger at the second fret, and use your ring finger for all fourth-fret notes and pinky for all fifth-fret notes.

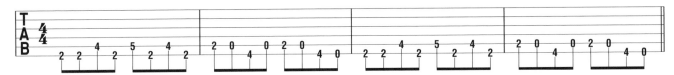

"ROCK OF AGES"
Words and Music by Joseph Elliott, Richard Allen, Stephen Clark, Richard Savage, Peter Willis and Robert John Lange

The riff below appears in the chorus of this monster hit. Place your fret hand in second position (so that your index finger is at the second fret) and assign one finger per fret. As for picking, use downstrokes for the first half of each measure (bars 1–2), then, beginning with a downstroke, use alternate picking for the second half (beats 3–4).

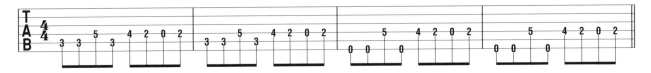

Rests and Repeats

As you're aware, music isn't made up solely of nonstop notes. There are often short bouts of silence from one or more instruments, and these are called **rests**. Like notes, rests can occur in many durations, including eighth rests, quarter rests, half rests, and whole rests. Each has its own musical symbol, shown below. Rests take up musical time, so you include them when counting, "1–2–3–4."

Counting Rests and Playing

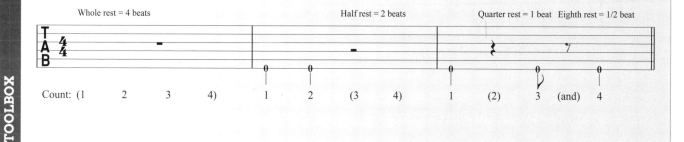

Sometimes in sheet music, including rhythm tab, we use shortcuts to indicate that a certain phrase should be repeated. The **repeat sign** symbols are indicated below. When you see these symbols, you play everything between them, and then repeat it one time.

Playing Repeats

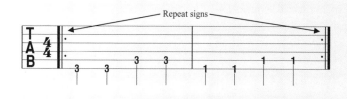

"AQUALUNG"

Words and Music by Ian Anderson and Jennie Anderson

For this riff, we're going to move up the neck to 3rd position; that is, your index finger should be at the third fret, with your remaining fret-hand fingers each getting the next successive fret location. As a result, the first note of the riff will be played using your ring finger on the 5th string at the fifth fret. Also, you'll notice that measures 2 and 4 don't have any notes, but rather just a whole rest. Be sure to count the full four beats of those measures.

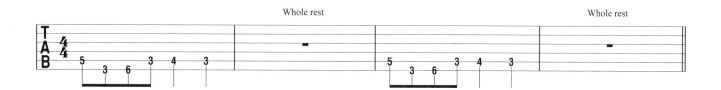

"25 OR 6 TO 4"
Words and Music by Robert Lamm

This classic riff is your first one to feature both quarter rests and repeat signs. Be sure to keep your rhythm count going through the rests. Begin the riff with your pinky finger on the fifth fret.

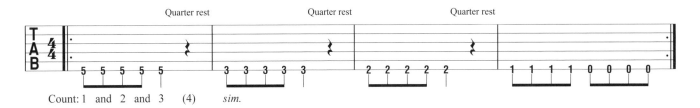

"OH, PRETTY WOMAN"
Words and Music by Roy Orbison and Bill Dees

This Roy Orbison gem is one of the greatest and most famous guitar riffs of all time. Use your ring finger for all fourth-fret notes and your index for all second-fret notes.

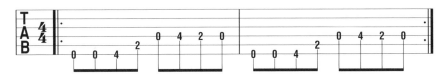

TOOLBOX

Ties

A **tie** is a small arc that connects two notes of the same pitch. When you come across two notes that are tied together, you play only the first note and then hold that note for the combined duration of both notes. For example, a quarter note tied to another quarter note gets two beats, a quarter note tied to an eighth note gets one and a half beats, and two eighth notes tied together get one beat. Ties most often connect notes across bar lines or notes from the first half to the second half of a measure.

Playing Ties

"I CAN'T HELP MYSELF
(SUGAR PIE, HONEY BUNCH)"
Words and Music by Brian Holland, Lamont Dozier and Edward Holland Jr.

This all-time classic R&B riff features a mid-measure tie connecting two eighth notes. Use your index and ring fingers on this one.

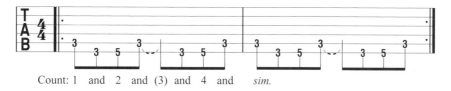

Count: 1 and 2 and (3) and 4 and   *sim.*

"DAY TRIPPER"
Words and Music by John Lennon and Paul McCartney

Another must-know riffs for the ages, anchor your index finger at the second fret and assign one finger per fret to play it most efficiently. Watch for the ties!

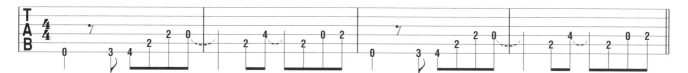

This Tom Petty classic is an uptempo rocker with a memorable single-string riff and lots of strumming. Begin in fifth position so that your ring, middle, and index fingers cover frets 7, 6, and 5, respectively, then shift down to play the third-fret G note with your index as well.

"Runnin' Down a Dream" appears on the next page to allow for easier reading.

"Runnin' Down a Dream"

Words and Music by Tom Petty, Jeff Lynne and Mike Campbell

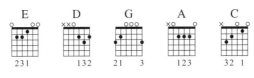

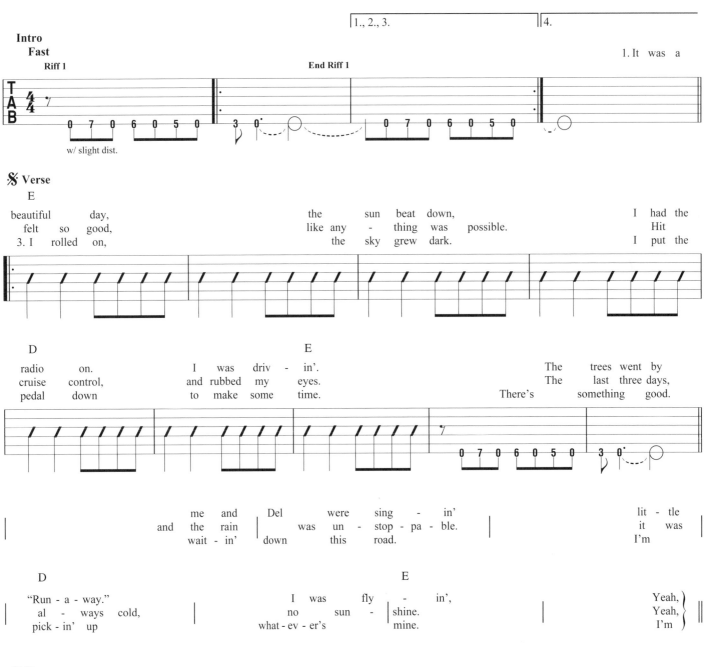

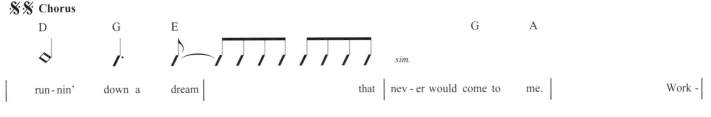

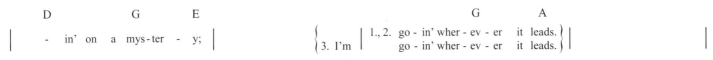

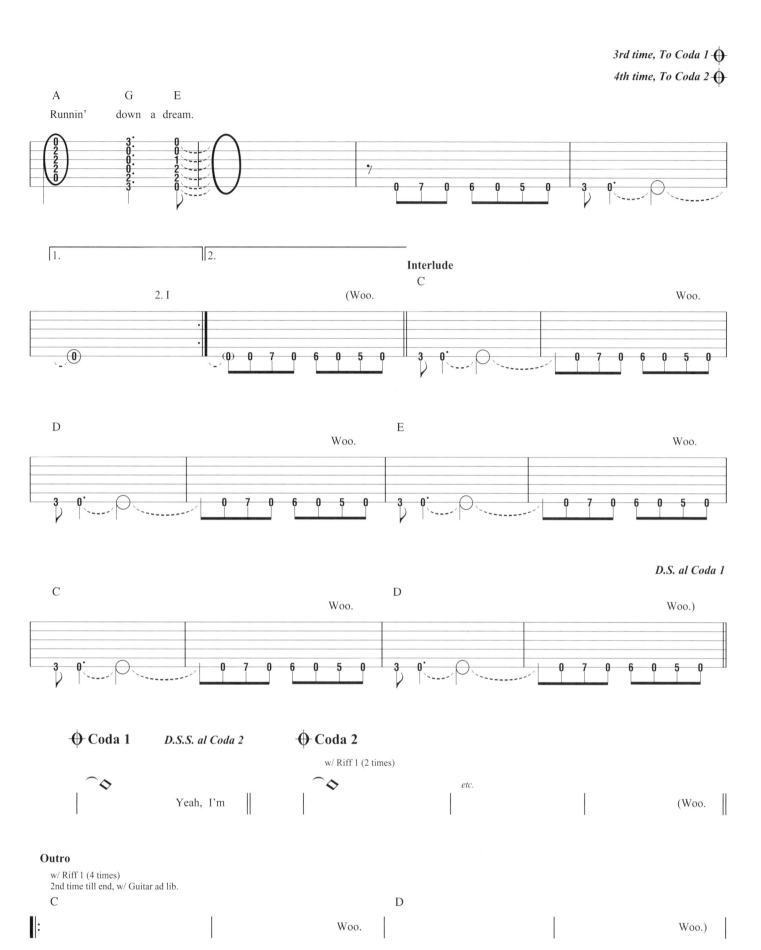

Chapter 5 ▶
Power Chords

In this chapter, you'll learn how to play power chords as well as a few new items and techniques for your Toolbox.

Power Chords

One of the most commonly used chord types in rock 'n' roll history, the **power chord** is as easy to play as it is omni-present. A power chord consists of just two notes; the lower-pitched note is the root for which the chord is named, and the higher note is the **5th**, which is why power chord names include the numeric suffix "5."

The first three power chords you'll learn are the ones that have an open string as its root: E5, A5, and D5.

As you can see, it only takes one finger to play these open-position power chords; however, it's a little trickier than it looks, as you need to mute the other four strings. For all three chords, the higher-pitched strings are muted by laying your index finger across them. For the A5 and D5 chords, focus on attacking just the indicated strings with your pick. It comes pretty quickly with practice.

Let's try some riffs using these three chords. This first one is in the key of A and uses eighth notes and quarter rests to give it a punchy rock feel.

Fig. 45 🔊

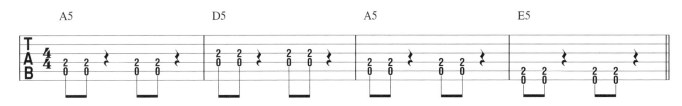

Here's an example in the key of E that you might hear as an intro or interlude in a hard rock classic.

Fig. 46 🔊

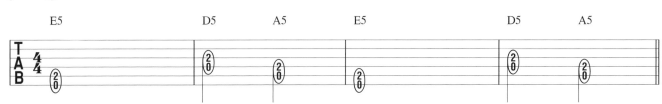

Palm Muting

The **palm mute** technique is one where you gently lay your pick hand's palm across the strings while playing so that the notes still sound but are slightly muted. This is a very popular technique in the context of power chords, especially in progressions with steady eighth-note rhythms.

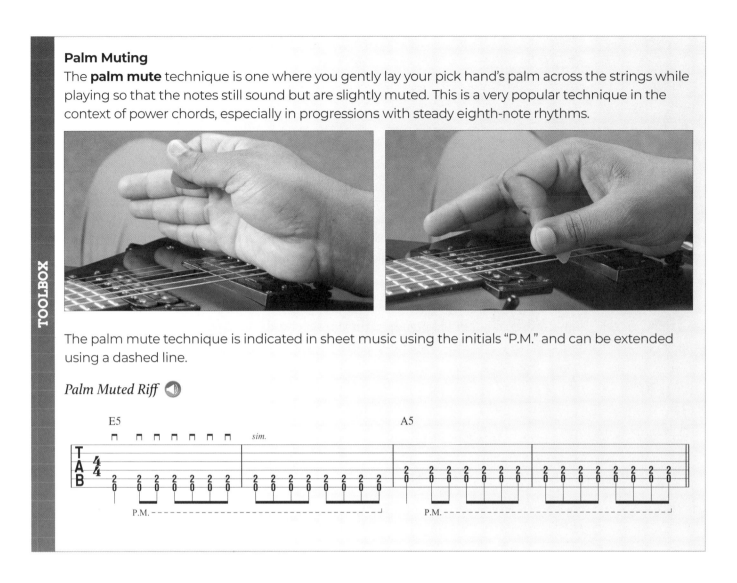

The palm mute technique is indicated in sheet music using the initials "P.M." and can be extended using a dashed line.

Palm Muted Riff

Movable Power Chords

In addition to the three open-position power chords, there are **movable** power chords that can be, well, *moved* anywhere along the fretboard, with the root changing based on the location of your fret hand's index finger. Use your ring finger for the "5," or higher-pitched note of the power chord. Although movable power chords can be found on any string pairs, the most common ones have 6th- or 5th-string roots.

Movable 6th-String Root   Movable 5th-String Root

Here are the names of all the movable power chords on the first 12 frets. (*Note/chord names repeat at fret 12; that is, the open 6th string is an E note, as the fretted 12th fret. Likewise, the first fret on the 6th string is an F, as is the 13th fret.)

Fig. 47

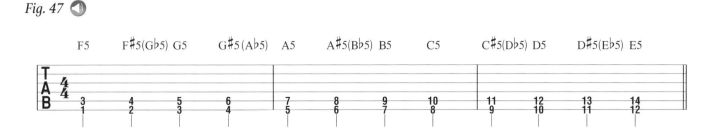

Fig. 48

You probably noticed that some chords have two names, one with a **sharp** symbol (#) and one with a **flat** symbol (♭), separated by a parentheses. When two notes—or chords, in this case—sound exactly the same but can be called by two names, we call them **enharmonic equivalents**. You don't need to know *why* this occurs right now—it has to do with what key the chord is in—but just understand that a power chord at the first fret with a 5th-string root can be called either a B♭5 or an A#5.

Let's try a few riffs using a mix of movable and open-position power chords.

Fig. 49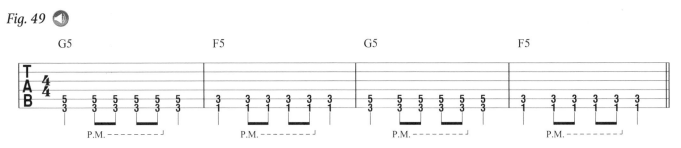

This riff, set here in the key of E, is emblematic of those heard in many rock and pop hits.

Fig. 50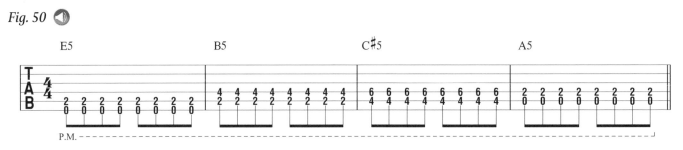

This riff features power chords that come in on the "and" of beats 2 and 4. This type of feel is called **syncopation** and is a very effective musical tool. Be sure you count your rhythm in eighth notes (i.e., 1–and–2–and–3–and–4–and).

Fig. 51

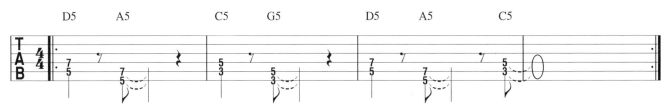

This next one is a heavy metal-style riff that alternates power chords with palm-muted, open 6th-string E notes.

Fig. 52

This classic rock-style riff uses rests, a touch of syncopation, and a slick, single-note **walking bass line** to lead back to the start of the riff. Use your middle and ring fingers for the single notes at the third and fourth frets, respectively.

Fig. 53

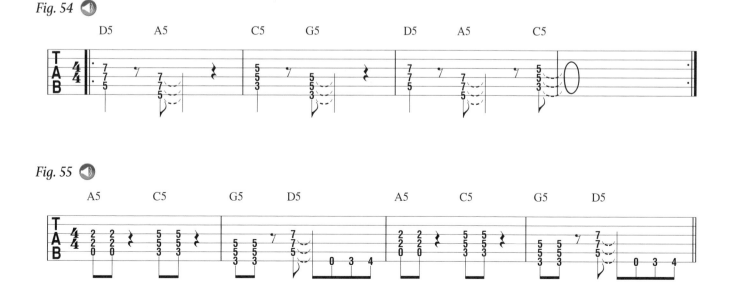

Three-Note Power Chords

In addition to the two-note power chords you've just learned, there's an alternative **three-note** version that adds the octave of the root note. Here are the shapes for the three-note versions of the open E5, A5, and D5 power chords as well as the 6th- and 5th-string root movable ones.

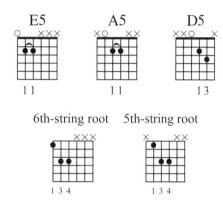

As you can see, these shapes are exactly like the two-note versions, except there's an added note—the octave of the root—on the next higher string. So, for example, the notes of the E5 chord are, from low to high, E–B–E, and the notes of the A5 chord are, also from low to high, A–E–A.

You also may have noticed that for E5 and A5, you'll need to barre your index finger across two strings, similarly to when you learned the F major chord. Even if you had trouble with the F chord, take solace in knowing that these are much easier, since there are no other fingers involved.

Let's replay a couple of the riffs above (Figs. 51 and 53) using a mixture of these open-position and movable three-note power chord shapes.

Fig. 54

Fig. 55

Did you notice a difference in the sound? The addition of the octave gives the chords and thus the riff a bigger, fuller sound that is often more desirable when you have power chords that get to ring out a bit. Conversely, adding the octave in a riff like the ones in Figs. 51 and 53, where the power chords are palm muted or moving at a faster tempo, doesn't really offer enough benefit.

TOOLBOX

Inverted Power Chords

Whoa! Upside-down power chords? Well, yes—sort of. An **inverted power chord** simply takes the root and the 5th and reverses them so that the 5th is the lower note. The easiest way to see this is to take the three-note power chord shape you just learned, eliminate the lowest note, and just play the two remaining notes.

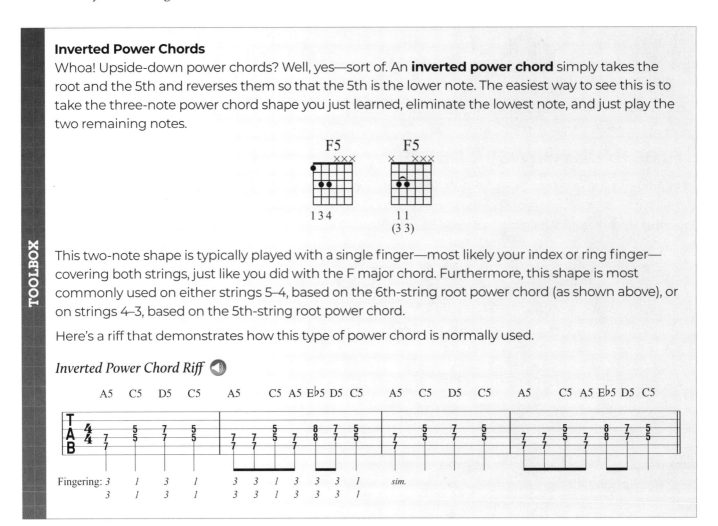

This two-note shape is typically played with a single finger—most likely your index or ring finger—covering both strings, just like you did with the F major chord. Furthermore, this shape is most commonly used on either strings 5–4, based on the 6th-string root power chord (as shown above), or on strings 4–3, based on the 5th-string root power chord.

Here's a riff that demonstrates how this type of power chord is normally used.

Inverted Power Chord Riff

Jam Time

Over the next couple of pages, you'll play a just a small sample of the myriad classic riffs composed of open-position and movable power chords, using both two- and three-note versions.

"ALL THE SMALL THINGS"
Words and Music by Tom DeLonge, Travis Barker and Mark Hoppus

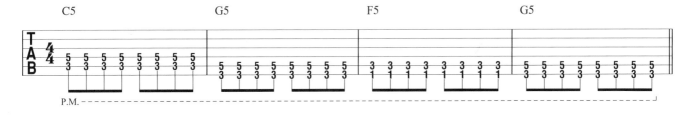

"JESSIE'S GIRL"

Words and Music by Rick Springfield

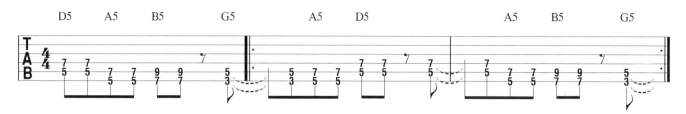

Dots and Slides

When you see a small dot immediately to the right of a note, it means that you should extend that note by half its value. For example, a **dotted quarter note** lasts for one and half beats, and a **dotted half note** lasts for three beats.

Dotted Rhythms

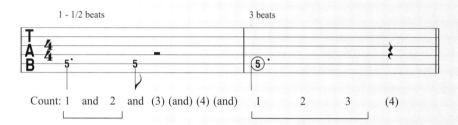

Not to be confused with "slide guitar," which is a guitar style worthy of its own book, the **slide** we're discussing here is an essential guitar technique commonly used in conjunction with power chords and single-note phrases. We're going to examine them here using power chords, but when you see them later in this book with single notes, the same rules apply.

There are three types of slide moves that guitarists use. The first is the "slide to or from nowhere," which can occur either before the target power chord (slide *from* nowhere) or immediately following a power chord (slide *to* nowhere). Generally speaking, the slide from nowhere starts *below* the target power chord and moves up the neck to it. The slide to nowhere typically involves sliding the power chord shape down the neck (towards the nut). These slides are indicated in rhythm tab with short "slash" lines leading to or from the tab numbers. You most often hear the latter at the end of a song, but it also occurs in power chord riffs prior to a rest.

Slide To/From Nowhere

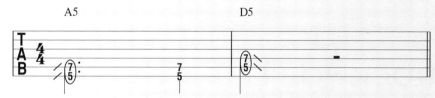

The second type of slide is one that connects two power chords (or notes), where both power chords are struck. Think of the sliding motion and pick attack of the second chord occurring simultaneously.

Picked Slide

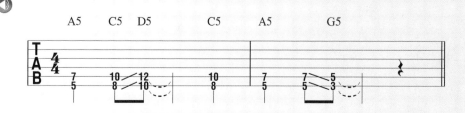

51

The third type of slide is one that connects two power chords (or notes), but only the first chord is struck. This also called a *legato slide*.

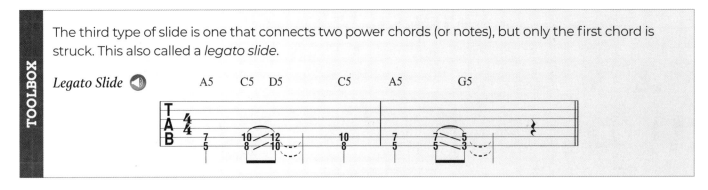

Legato Slide

OK, back to jamming on some all-time great power-chord riffs. Some of these will feature the dotted notes and slides you just learned, so pay attention.

"T.N.T."
Words and Music by Angus Young, Malcolm Young and Bon Scott

AC/DC may very well be the kings of open-position power chords. For this one, use your middle finger for the G notes on the 6th string at the third fret.

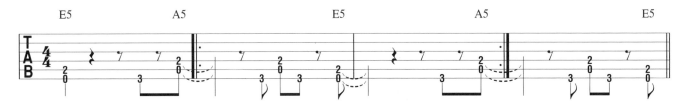

"I HATE MYSELF FOR LOVING YOU"
Words and Music by Desmond Child and Joan Jett

This riff features three-note power chords, with a short single-note line in the middle. When you reach those single notes, your fret hand will be in perfect position to play the fifth-fret D notes with your index finger and the seventh-fret B notes with your ring finger.

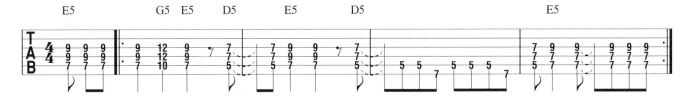

"ROCK YOU LIKE A HURRICANE"
Words and Music by Rudolf Schenker, Klaus Meine and Herman Rarebell

Here's another classic hard rock riff featuring three-note power chords plus one of those cool descending "slides to nowhere."

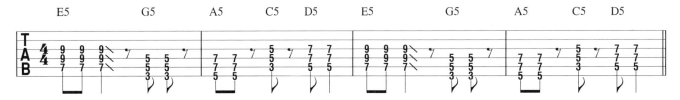

"OWNER OF A LONELY HEART"

Words and Music by Trevor Rabin, Jon Anderson, Chris Squire and Trevor Horn

The intro to Yes's 1986 smash hit features not only three-note power chords but also dotted quarter notes and your first **double tie**, where three note values are all tied together. Plus, you'll throw in a little slide to nowhere when the double-tied D5 chord ends.

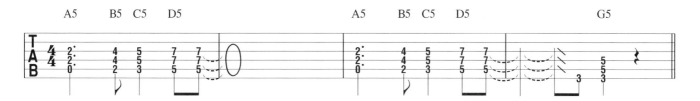

"WORKING FOR THE WEEKEND"

Words and Music by Paul Dean, Matthew Frenette and Michael Reno

This riff offers a slight twist on the power chord. It begins on a standard B5 power chord, for which you should use your index and ring fingers as usual, but soon switches things up a bit. At beat 3, you'll remove your ring finger from the fourth fret on string 4 and instead place your middle finger at the third fret. Then, on the final eighth note of the measure ("and" of beat 4), you'll need to barre your index finger across strings 5–4 for that inverted power chord. It's best to have all three fingers in position at the start, then simply lift them off in descending order when the time comes. You'll see that a cool single-note riff offsets the power chords. Use your index and middle fingers for the notes at the first and second frets, respectively.

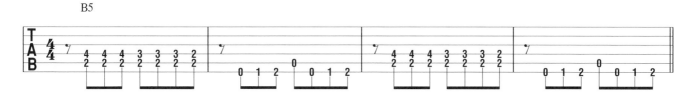

Featuring arguably the most famous and recognizable guitar riff of all time, this 1972 classic by Deep Purple has proven to be truly timeless. The main riff comprises inverted power chords, while the verses feature three-note versions played one note at a time, and the chorus use three-note versions held for entire measures as well as a short motif using inverted power chords. Use your index and ring fingers exclusively for the inverted power chords, shifting your hand position as needed.

> "Smoke on the Water" appears on the next page to allow for easier reading.

"SMOKE ON THE WATER"

Words and Music by Ritchie Blackmore, Ian Gillan, Roger Glover, Jon Lord and Ian Paice

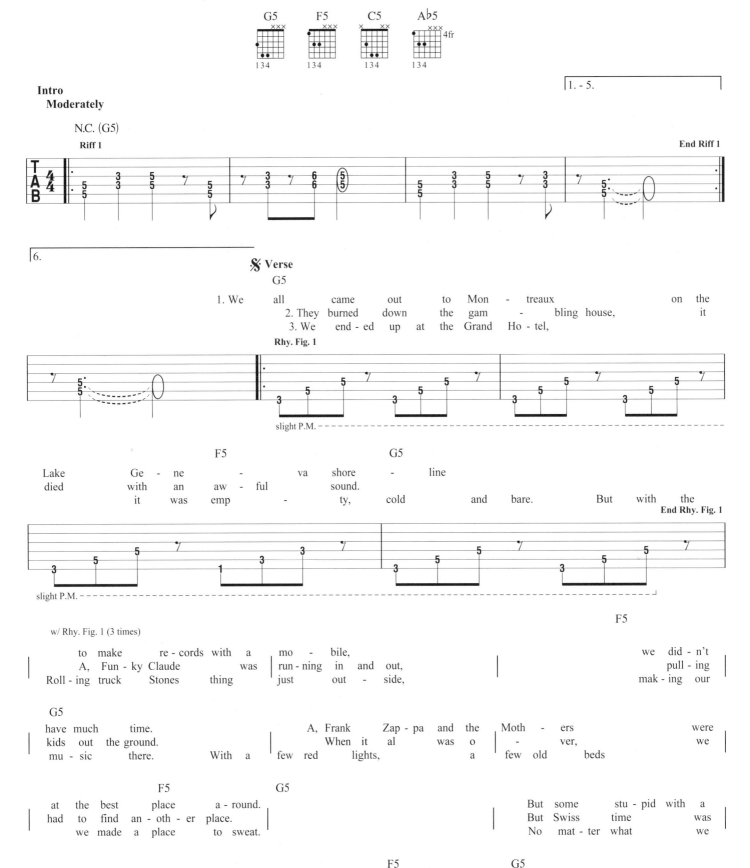

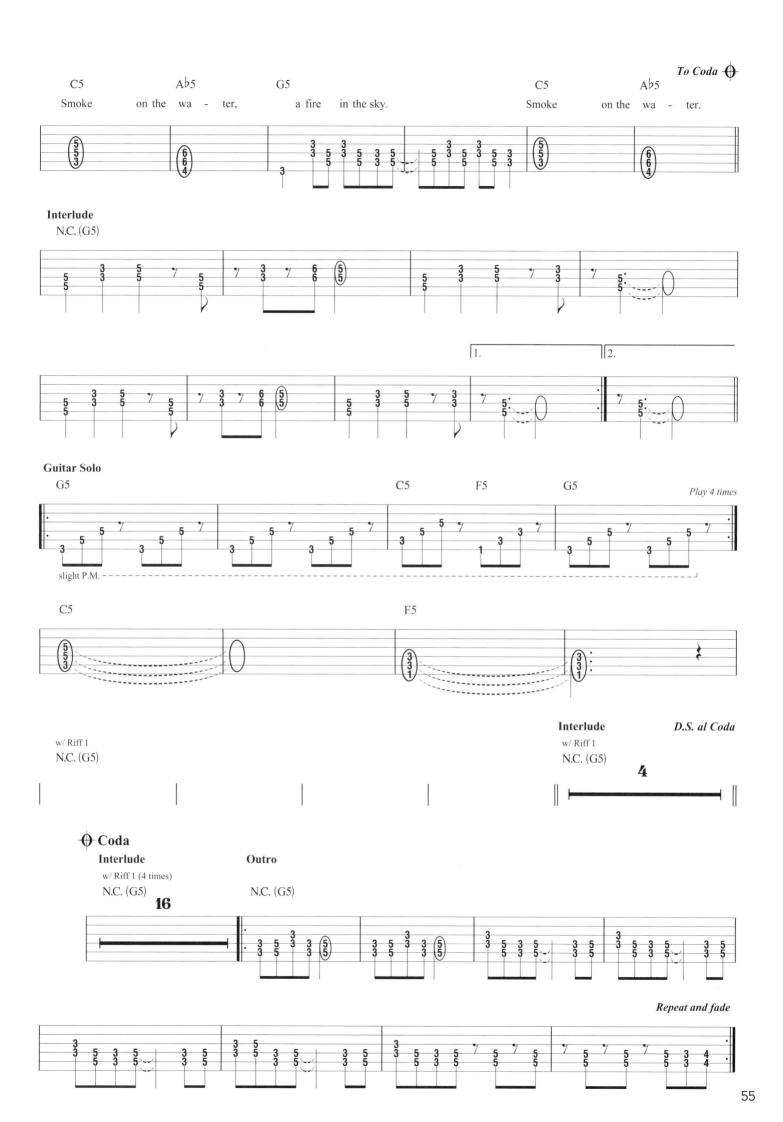

Chapter 6 ▶️
Arpeggios

In this chapter, you'll learn a new way of playing chords and add a few new items to your Toolbox.

Arpeggios

Up until this point, when playing chords, you've only strummed them. But you can also play chords one note at a time. A chord played in this manner is called an **arpeggio**. Let's take a look at a C major arpeggio played in both ascending (from low to high in pitch) and descending fashion. Use downstrokes for the first four notes, then up-strokes for the next four, ending with a downstroke on the root, C. Keep holding the chord shape down while you play, letting each note continue to ring together.

Fig. 56 🔊

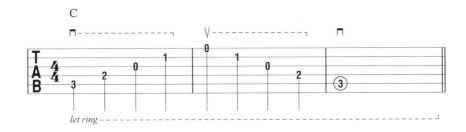

Now, let's try it again, but this time we'll add a simple chord change.

Fig. 57 🔊

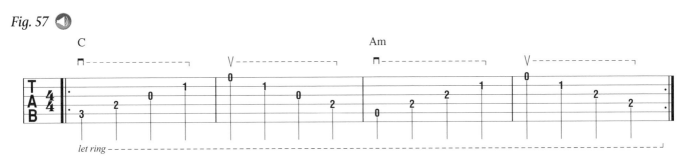

Though it was important to generate clean-sounding chords—where all the notes ring out clearly—while strumming, it's even more crucial when playing arpeggios. If you're having any trouble with muted notes, check to make sure your fret-hand fingers are properly arched so that they're no inadvertently muting other strings.

The C and Am arpeggios occur over five strings, which makes going up and down the chord very convenient in a quarter- or eighth-note rhythm in 4/4 time. For chords that cover all six strings, you sometimes need to choose which notes you're going to include, and if you're playing an ascending-descending pattern, where you're going to "turn it around." Here, there are no hard, steadfast rules—it's largely up to your creative whims—but one common strategy is to play the highest-pitched note on downbeat of measure 2, or on beat 3, if you're using an eighth-note rhythm. In the example below, use the same picking pattern as before.

Fig. 58 🔊

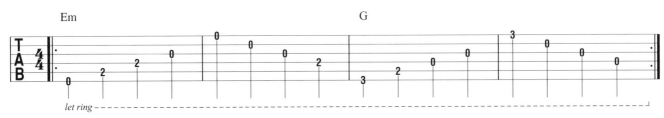

A chord that uses only four strings, like D, Dm, or F, presents its own challenge in an ascending-descending pattern. Here's one common strategy. Like the six-string chords above, the pattern is arranged so that the highest-pitched note falls either on the downbeat of the second measure or on beat 3 when using an eighth-note rhythm. Pay close attention to the picking directions.

Fig. 59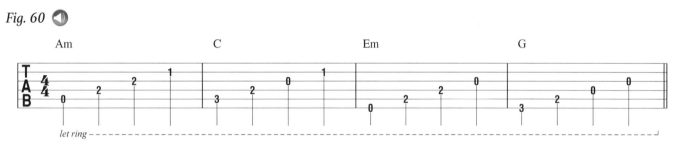

Of course, not all arpeggios are played in an ascending-descending manner. Sometimes, you will encounter a series of ascending-only arpeggios.

Fig. 60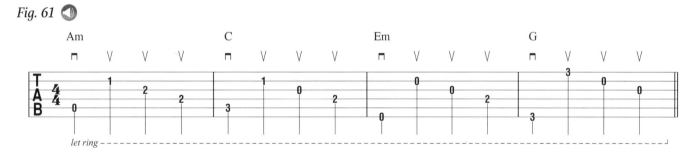

Or, conversely, you might come across a progression with only descending arpeggios, or similarly and more commonly, where each chord begins on its low root but then jumps to a higher note and descends, such as this riff.

Fig. 61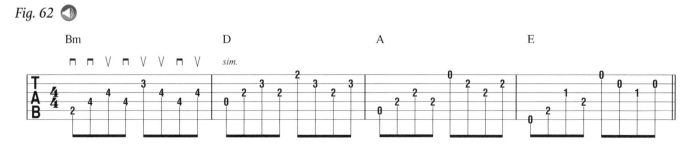

These are just a few basic arpeggio patterns. The possibilities pretty much are limited to your creative ambition. As such, it's not feasible to present all the possible patterns here. Instead, practice the ones shown here, as well as the more complex variation below, and try them with various other chord progressions, too. And when you're comfortable with the basic technique, begin experimenting with patterns of your own.

This riff features four-, five-, and six-string chords, but there are still consistent features in the pattern, such as always playing the highest-pitched note on beat 3 of the measure and the picking pattern itself. Use the pick direction indicators above the first measure for all four chords.

Fig. 62

TOOLBOX

Slash Chords

No, we're not talking about chords used exclusively by Guns N' Roses guitarist Slash, but rather a chord with a note other than its root as the bass, or lowest-sounding, note. For example, the D major chord you learned has the open D string, or the chord root, as the lowest-sounding note. But the D major chord contains three notes—D, F#, and A—and any one of those notes can serve as the bass note, while the root remains D. When one of the other chord tones serves as the bass note, we indicate that by first writing the chord root followed by a forward slash and the name of the bass note. So a D/F# chord is a D major chord with the F# note "in the bass," or as the lowest pitch of the chord. The D/A chord is a D major chord with an A note in the bass. Below are the chord frames for each of these.

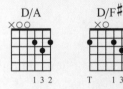

The D/A is quite easy, as all you need to do is add the open A string to the chord, muting the 6th string. The D/F#, however, requires a new technique: thumb-fretting. To do this, fret the D major chord as you normally would, but instead of keeping your fret hand's thumb behind the neck, wrap it around to hold down the 6th string at the second fret, allowing the tip to touch, and thus mute, the 5th string, if possible. Try these new chord shapes out in the arpeggio riff below.

Slash Chord Arpeggio Riff

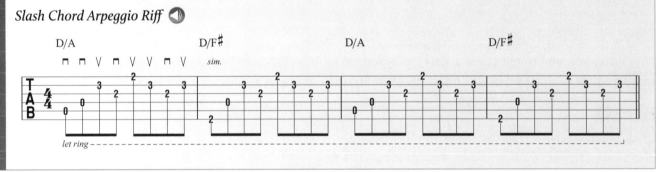

Jam Time

Let's play through some riffs that feature arpeggios in various forms. You might come across new patterns or even some chords that are slightly altered, but if you follow the tab and the accompanying instructions, you'll do great.

"DON'T FEAR THE REAPER"
Words and Music by Donald Roeser

This classic rock riff cycles through Am, G, and F chords with a twist, namely that every chord ends on the open G note whether it's part of the chord or not. Use downstrokes for the first three notes of each arpeggio and an up-stroke on the open G string. For the F chord, use the two-note power chord shape but arch your fingers enough so that the 4th string (D) is allowed to ring clearly.

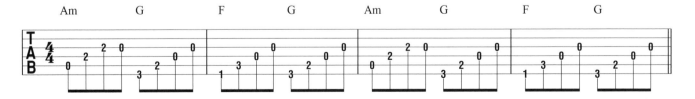

"LAST KISS"
Words and Music by Wayne Cochran

This ode to the doo-wop sound of the 1950s features tied notes in each arpeggio. Remember that you only play the first of the two tied notes but hold it for their combined duration.

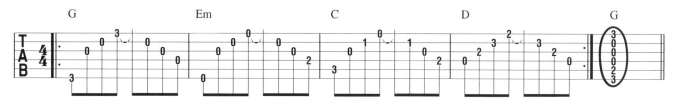

"THINKING OUT LOUD"
Words and Music by Ed Sheeran and Amy Wadge

In this old-school, R&B-style ballad, Ed Sheeran builds a cool bass line within his chord voicings. Watch for the dotted quarter notes.

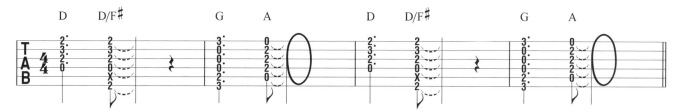

TOOLBOX

6/8 Time

Although there are many possible time signatures, there are only a few that are commonly heard in popular music, be it rock, pop, country, blues, or soul. Not surprisingly, 4/4 is by *far* the most common time signature, which is why everything you've learned so far has been in 4/4. Another one that you'll hear frequently is 6/8. Considered to have a "lilting" feel, the 6/8 time signature indicates that there are six beats per measure, and an eighth note receives the beat. However, it's also generally *felt* as a two-pulse measure, where beats 1 and 4 get the pulse. So you'd count it as, "**1**–2–3–**4**–5–6," sort of accenting the 1 and 4.

6/8 Arpeggio Riff

"EVERYBODY HURTS"

Words and Music by William Berry, Peter Buck, Michael Mills and Michael Stipe

This ballad from R.E.M. is in 6/8 time and uses consecutive downstrokes when ascending the chord and upstrokes when descending it. You'll count, "1–2–3–4–5–6," but give added emphasis to beats 1 and 4, thus splitting each measure into two "pulses."

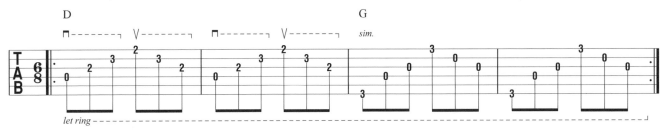

"HALLELUJAH"

Words and Music by Leonard Cohen

Widely recognized as one of the greatest songs ever written, this Leonard Cohen masterpiece features arpeggios set in 6/8 time. Beat 4 of each measure features a partial chord, where you'll strum the top three strings of the G and Em chords, respectively, rather than a single note. Notice too that the final beat of each measure is a F♯ note, which serves as a **leading** tone to the next chord root. As for picking pattern, experiment with what feels most comfortable to you. Because the tempo is fairly slow, you might find using all downstrokes to be the easiest.

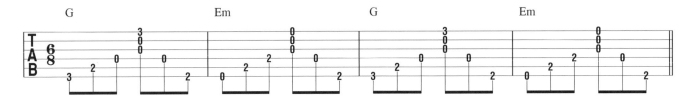

TOOLBOX

The Other G Chord

Occasionally, you'll see a chord you've already learned but with a different note arrangement and fingering. Below, you'll find a very popular alternative to the open G chord you already know; in fact, this one is even more widely used. The only difference is that this new shape has a fretted D note on the 2nd string at the third fret. Use your ring finger for this new note, and drop your pinky down on the 1st string, third fret.

G

2 1   3 4

"NOBODY'S FOOL"

Words and Music by Tom Keifer

Let's try out that new G chord shape in this 1980s power ballad by Cinderella.

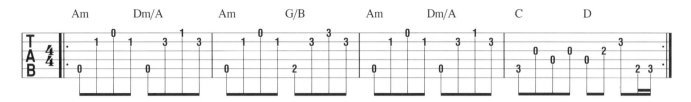

To close out Chapter 6, we will play the classic Eric Clapton song "Wonderful Tonight." This touching love song about waiting for his girlfriend (and later, wife) Pattie Boyd to get ready for a night out has one of the most distinctive guitar riffs of the 1970s and some gorgeous arpeggios to go with it.

"Wonderful Tonight" appears on the next page to allow for easier reading.

"WONDERFUL TONIGHT"

Words and Music by Eric Clapton

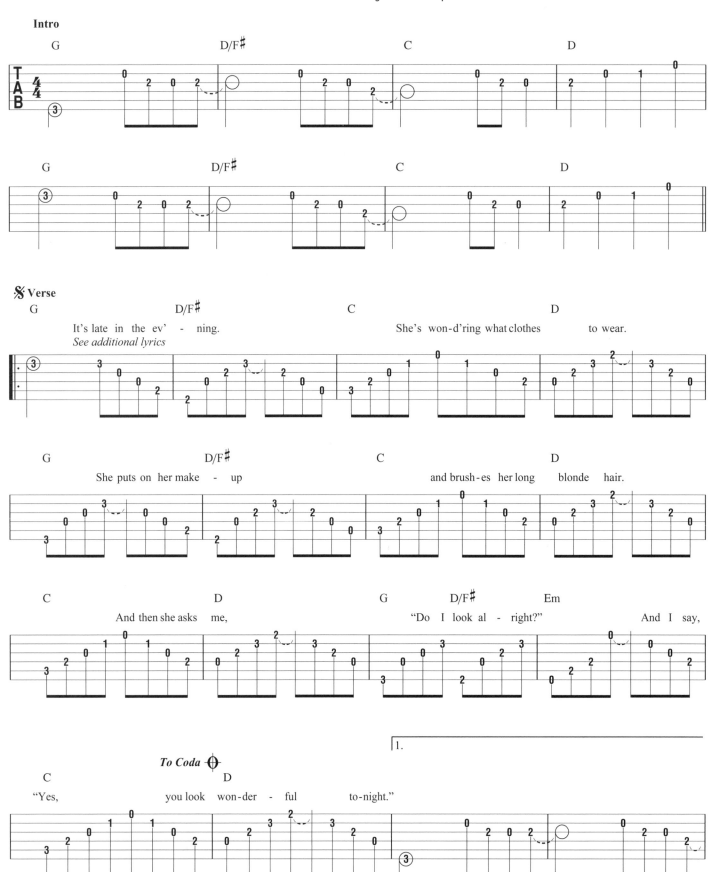

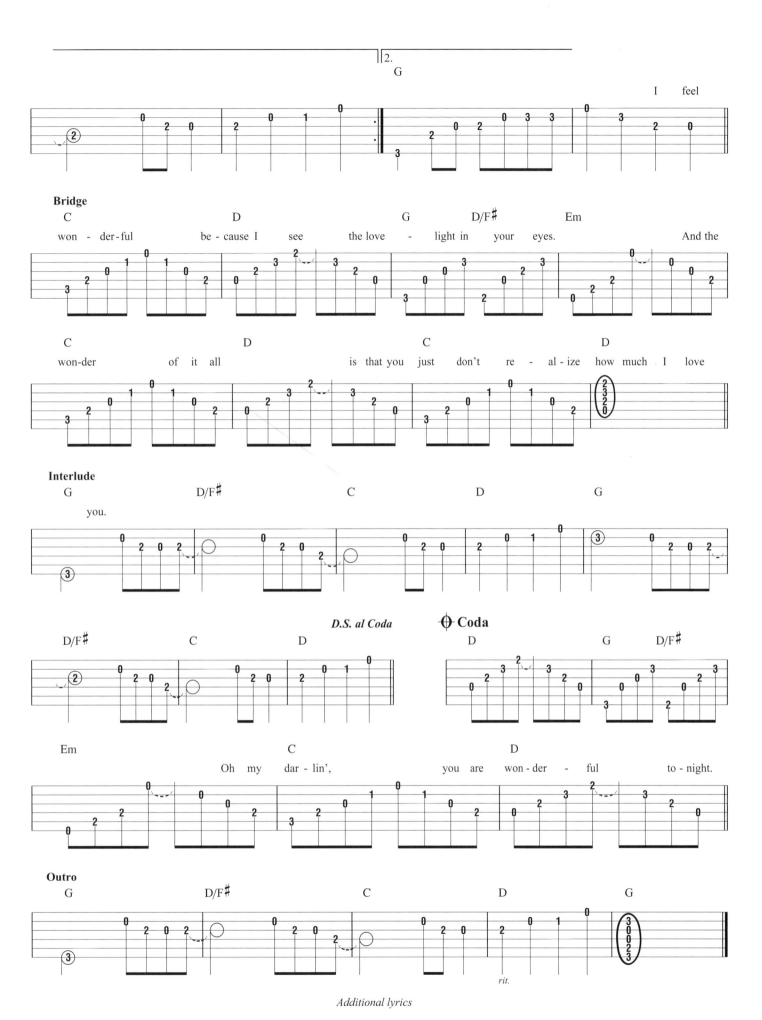

Additional lyrics

2. We go to a party, and ev'ryone turns to see
   This beautiful lady that's walking around with me.
   And then she asks me, "Do you feel alright?"
   And I say, "Yes, I feel wonderful tonight."

3. It's time to go home now, and I've got an aching head.
   So I give her the car keys and she helps me to bed.
   And then I tell her, as I torn out the light,
   I say, "My darling, you were wonderful tonight."

Chapter 7 ▶

Fingerstyle

In this chapter, you're going to put the pick away and let your fingers do the talking. While last chapter's chord arpeggios are fresh, you'll learn basic fingerpicking patterns, the 16th-note rhythm, and some new items for your Toolbox.

Fingerstyle Guitar

Though the guitar pick is a wonderful tool, the ability to play guitar fingerstyle is an indispensable skill. *Fingerstyle* guitar technique typically calls for your thumb to pluck notes on strings 6–4, while your index, middle, and ring fingers handle duties on strings 3, 2, and 1, respectively. Of course, there are many exceptions, but the good news is that it's generally pretty easy to identify when you should change your fingering pattern. Still, we'll point them out when they arise in the exercises to follow.

In fingerstyle guitar, we use letters *p–i–m–a* to identify which pick-hand fingers to use: *p* = thumb, *i* = index, *m* = middle, and *a* = ring. At rest but ready to play fingerstyle, your hand should look like this:

Let's try a very basic ascending and descending fingerpicking pattern using only the open strings of an Em chord. Let all the notes ring throughout the exercise.

Fig. 63 ◀

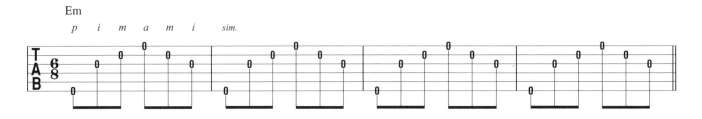

And now we'll add a chord change to make the progression Em–G, keeping the same fingerpicking pattern.

Fig. 64 ◀

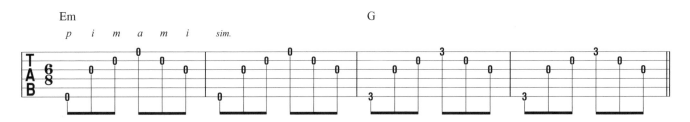

As you pluck through these arpeggios, keep your picking hand relaxed, move your fingers as little as possible, and let all the notes ring throughout.

Now let's try an ascending-only arpeggio pattern for an A–E–D chord progression. This selection of chords will require you to shift your picking hand to different string sets.

Fig. 65

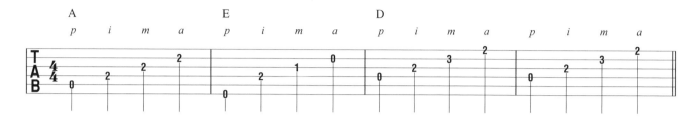

Likewise, you'll also find descending arpeggios, like this progression.

Fig. 66

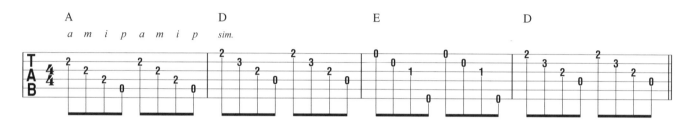

And like you saw with arpeggios in the previous chapter, you will come across patterns that begin with the root or other bass note followed immediately by the highest pitch and then descending the remainder of the chord.

Fig. 67

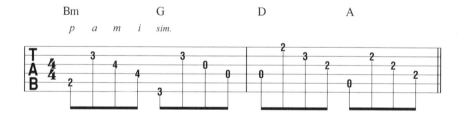

Here's another common pattern arpeggio pattern for fingerstyle guitar. Even though you're only playing four notes per chord, you're going to use your thumb on the lowest two played strings for each chord, to get used to moving your thumb from string to string, and your index and middle fingers on the other two notes. As a bonus, you'll get to use your fret-hand's thumb as well for the that D/F♯ chord. Thumbs at the ready, and go!

Fig. 68

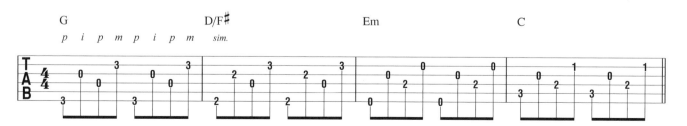

16th Notes

By now, you should have a pretty solid grasp on quarter- and eighth-note rhythms, not to mention half notes, whole notes, and maybe even dotted notes. So now it's time to introduce the **16th-note rhythm**, which, as you may have guessed, is what you get when you divide eighth notes in half, or quarter notes into four parts, or subdivisions. You count 16th notes like this: "1-ee-and-a, 2-ee-and-a," and so forth.

A beat containing 16th notes may comprise several variations or combinations of 16th notes, 16th rests, eighth notes, eighth rests, and dotted eighth notes or rests. The diagram below shows several possibilities using rests.

Fig. 69

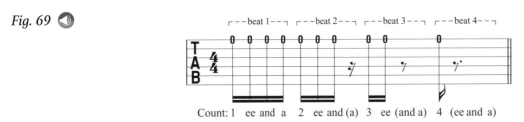

Aside from a full beat containing four 16th notes, the two 16th-note rhythms you'll encounter most frequently are the "eighth plus two 16ths" and "two 16ths plus an eighth."

Fig. 70

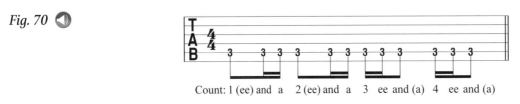

Now let's put these 16th-note rhythms into musical context with a fingerstyle progression. As you did previously, strive for an economy of motion and let the notes ring throughout.

Fig. 71

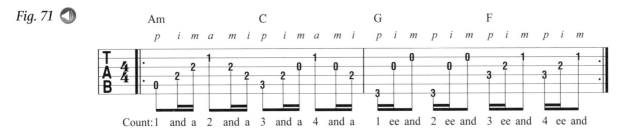

Here's a longer and "busier" progression that should really get your fingerpicking hand into a groove. Note the arpeggio pattern in the first three measures, where, for each chord, you ascend, descend, and then ascend one last note before the chord change. This is a popular pattern in fingerstyle guitar so it's well worth getting it comfortably under your fingers.

Fig. 72

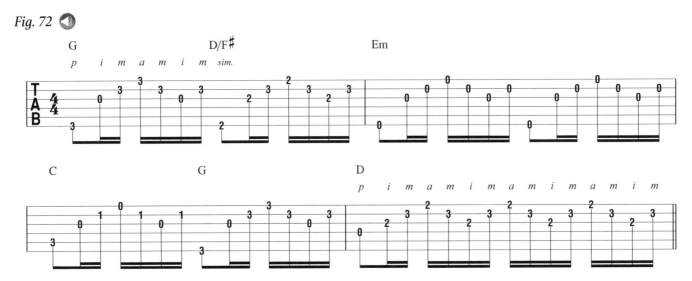

The next step in fingerstyle guitar is to pluck two notes simultaneously, using your thumb and one of your other fingers. In this introductory exercise, you'll use your thumb and middle finger together. Pay attention to the pick-hand fingers used in this pattern, as it's a combination you'll use abundantly in fingerstyle music.

Fig. 73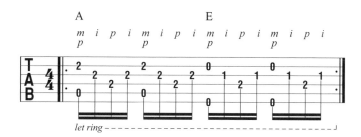

Now let's try the same basic fingerpicking technique, but vary the rhythm a bit. The rhythm presented in this ar-peggio riff is also one that you'll frequently encounter in fingerstyle guitar songs.

Fig. 74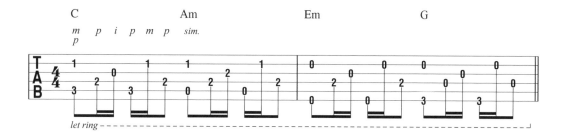

Travis Picking

Named for country superstar Merle Travis, the **Travis picking** technique entails syncopated melodic arpeggio tones (i.e., played on the "up" beats) played against a steady alternating bass line, typically comprising the root and 5th of the chord. The example below shows a slightly modified picking pattern from the usual one to help you get started.

Travis Picking Over A

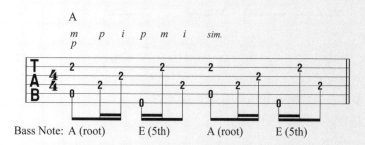

As you can see, this example features a bass line that alternates between A (the root) and E (the 5th) on the downbeats of the measure, while A major arpeggio tones (A, C♯, and E) fill in the space on the upbeats. Please note that the rhythm used here—though it is very common to Travis picking—is not an exclusive one. You'll find all sorts of rhythmic ideas employed for the arpeggios when using Travis picking, but that steady alternating bass line is the hallmark of the technique.

Let's try a Travis picking example in the key of A. Note that for the A and E chords, your thumb handles the notes on strings 4, 5, and 6. It might sound like a tough assignment, but you'll fall into the groove pretty quickly, as long as you start slowly and focus on hitting those bass notes on the downbeats. (For Bm, the thumb plucks strings 5 and 4.)

Fig. 75 🔊

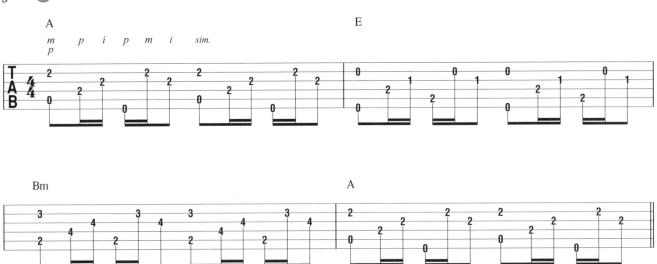

The shapes of chords like A, D, and E have their root notes and 5ths sort of "built in." But chords like C and F do not have both the root and 5th in a "bass" position. The solution to this issue when using Travis picking is to use these two new slash chords: C/G and F/C.

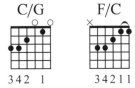

Let's try the basic Travis picking pattern (now in its full form) using just these two chords, so that your fret hand's fingers get used to the shapes.

Fig. 76 🔊

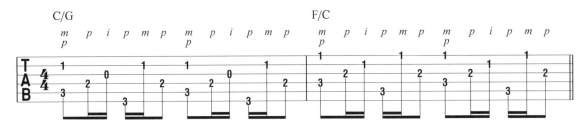

So far, you've been playing dyads (two notes together) on the first downbeat of each fingerpicking pattern; however, dyads can occur just about anywhere in a fingerstyle riff. In this next example, you'll use your middle and index fingers to simultaneously pluck two notes on adjacent strings on the "and" of beats 1 and 3. Note that your thumb will continue to play an alternating bass pattern.

Fig. 77 🔊

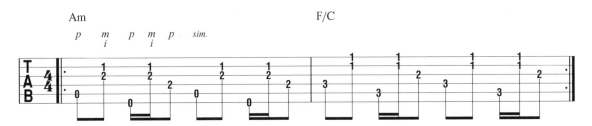

68

Now let's add two more chords to expand the riff.

Fig. 78

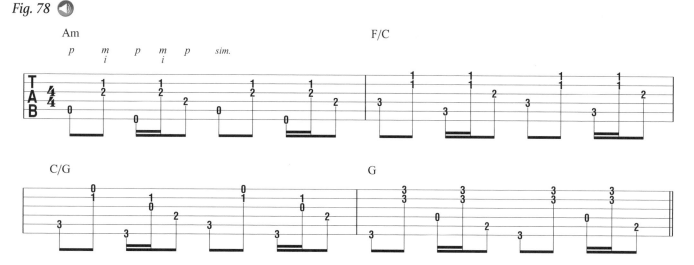

Jam Time

Time to put some of your fingerpicking skills to work on some real songs. A few of these examples will introduce some new ideas and even chord shapes, but if you follow the fingering suggestions provided, you'll do fine.

"LANDSLIDE"
Words and Music by Stevie Nicks

Guitarist Lindsey Buckingham created a truly timeless fingerpicking riff using this very basic pattern. Note that for the G/B chord, you can fret a full G chord; you'll just be playing the B note on the 5th string (second fret) as the lowest note.

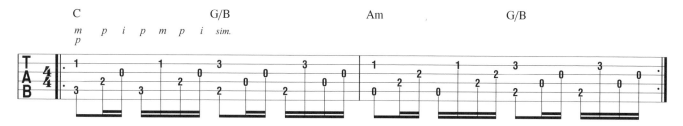

"WHEN THE CHILDREN CRY"
Words and Music by Mike Tramp and Vito Bratta

Here's the intro riff from this monster ballad by the 1980s hair metal band White Lion. This one's a little different in that rather than a chord progression, you're playing a melody on the 1st string against open-string notes from an Em chord.

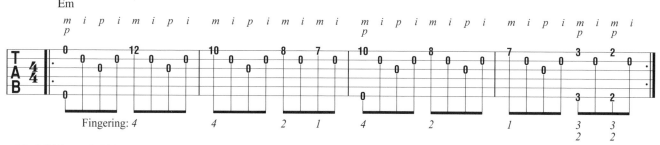

"SILENT LUCIDITY"
Words and Music by Chris DeGarmo

Here's another power ballad by from a 1980s hard rock band. Similar to "When the Children Cry," this verse riff requires you to play up the neck at the start. When you get to the E minor section at measure 3, your fret-hand's fingers will form a shape similar to the D major chord, only your index finger is planted on the 4th string at the second fret (E), and your ring finger only drops down on the 2nd string starting at beat 3. Follow the picking and fretting finger guides in the tab.

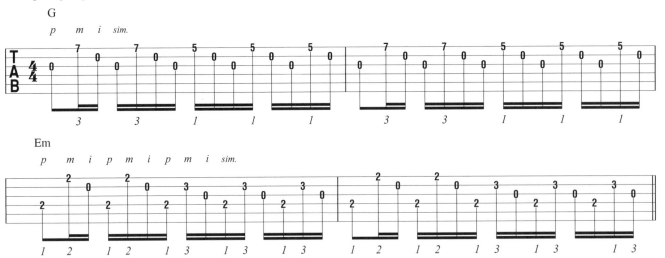

"YOU'VE GOT A FRIEND"
Words and Music by Carole King

James Taylor is a master of fingerstyle guitar. He's also very creative with his chord voicings, often altering a basic open major or minor chord by adding new notes to create beautiful sounds, as he does in the chorus to "You've Got a Friend," shown below. Use the fret-hand fingering suggestions to help you properly fret the chord shapes. (The asterisks indicate that chord labels refer to the overall harmony.)

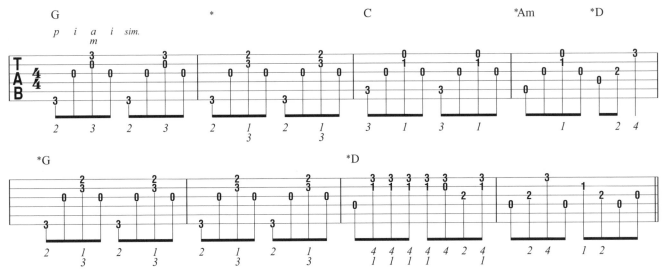

Widely considered one of the greatest fingerstyle acoustic guitar songs of all time, "Dust in the Wind" by Kansas is arranged here in an eighth-note Travis picking pattern that is simpler than the 16th-note driven original. The "hook" of this guitar part is the repeating C–B–D melody line on the 2nd string. Use your pinky finger for the D note at the third fret on the 2nd string whenever it appears in the main intro riff. Also watch for the slash chords—you know the D/F♯ chord, but the G/B should be played with your index on the 5th string at the second fret and your ring finger (or pinky) on the 2nd string at the third fret. For the Am/G chord, play a regular Am chord, but reach your pinky across the fretboard to fret the 6th string at the third fret.

"DUST IN THE WIND"

Words and Music by Kerry Livgren

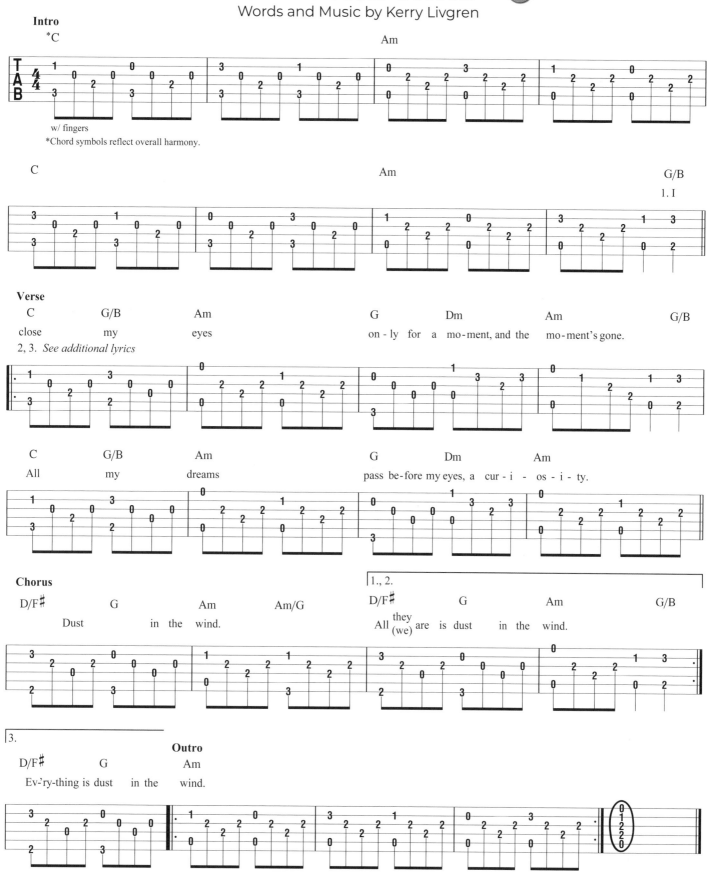

Additional Lyrics

2. Same old song,
   Just a drop of water in the endless sea.
   All we do
   Crumbles to the ground though we refuse to see.

3. Don't hang on,
   Nothing lasts forever but the earth and sky.
   It slips away,
   And all your money won't another minute buy.

Chapter 8 ▶

The Blues and 7th Chords

In this chapter, you'll learn the basics of the **blues**, including the 12-bar blues progression, the shuffle rhythm, the "5–6" shuffle pattern, and 7th chords.

The 12-Bar Blues Form

The standard blues progression, called the **12-bar blues** form, features just three chords—the I, IV, and V. You already learned a little about this when we discussed the keys of G major, D major, and A major early on in this book, and how certain chords fit into the key. If you'll recall, in the key of A, you had three major chords: A (the I chord), D (the IV chord), and E (the V chord).

In the blues, these three chords appear in a very specific pattern over the course of 12 measures, or bars, thus the name "12-bar blues." The I chord is played in bars 1–4, the IV chord in bars 5–6, the I chord again in bars 7–8, then the V chord in bar 9, the IV chord in bar 10, followed by the I chord in bar 11, and either the V or the I in bar 12.

Fig. 79 🔊

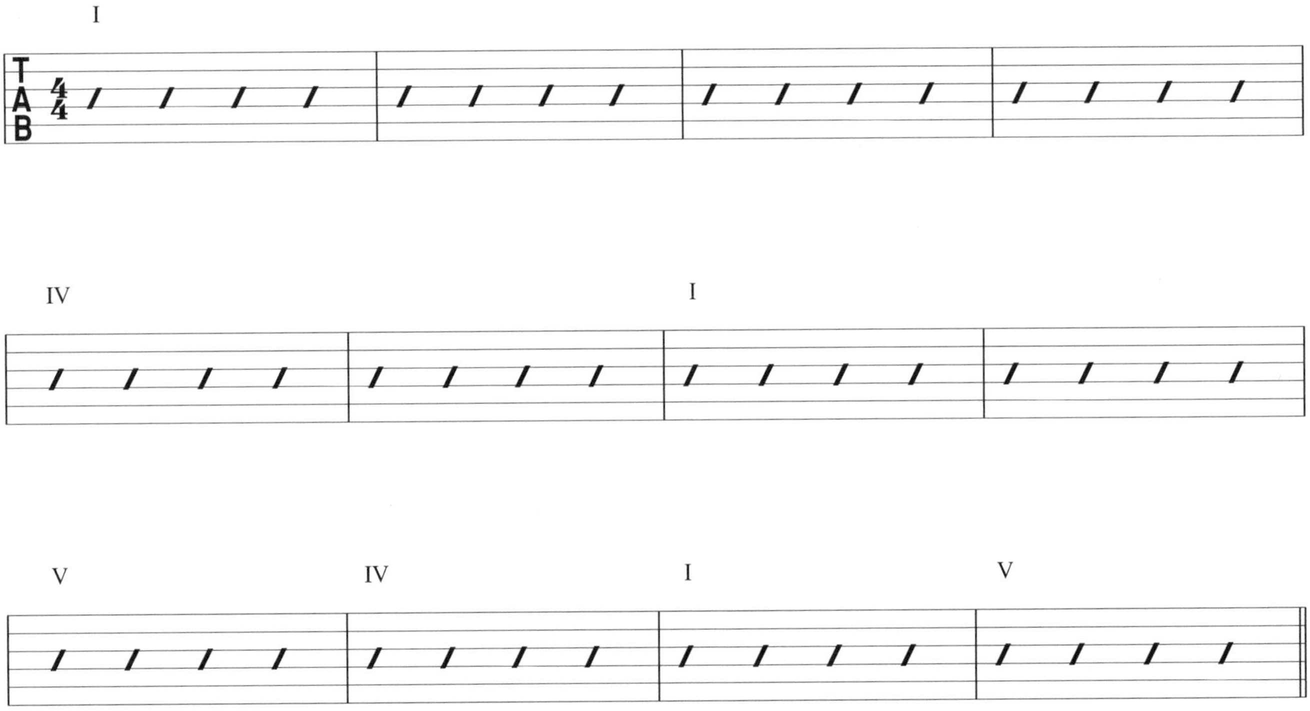

The Shuffle Rhythm

In addition to the form, the blues also has a definitive rhythmic feel called the **shuffle rhythm**. The shuffle is generally played in eighth notes and is best described as a pair of eighth notes where the first is played on the downbeat, as usual, but the second eighth note is slightly delayed, so that it's played about two-thirds of the way through the beat, rather than at the halfway mark like a regular eighth note. In sheet music, the shuffle rhythm is indicated either with the words "shuffle feel" or with the following symbol:

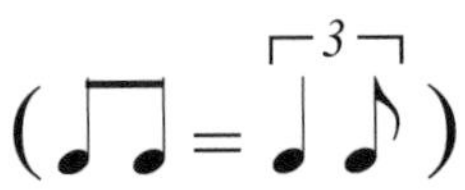

$$\left(\quad \sqcap \quad = \quad \overset{\ulcorner 3 \urcorner}{\sqcap} \quad \right)$$

Triplets

To help you better understand the "math" behind the shuffle rhythm, now is a good time to learn the *triplet* rhythm. The eighth-note triplet, which is the most common type, is a quarter note divided into three equal subdivisions. So in 4/4 time, you count eighth-note triplets like this: "**1**–and–uh, **2**–and–uh, **3**–and–uh, **4**–and–uh. In the rhythm tab, an eighth-note triplet appears as three eighth notes beamed together, with a small number "3" at the center.

Eighth-Note Triplets

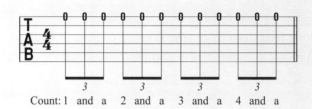

To create the shuffle rhythm, you basically play the downbeat (1, 2, 3, and 4) and the "uh," or third note of the triplet, while skipping the "and" completely.

Depending on the song, you might allow the downbeat note to ring right up until the "uh" note, or you might mute it right away so that the "and" portion is silent; for example, you'll get more of the latter when using the palm muting technique.

Shuffle Rhythm

Keep in mind that the rhythm will be written as eighth notes with a "shuffle feel" instruction at the beginning, as it's much easier to read. We broke the triplets up in this manner just to better demonstrate how you arrive at the shuffle feel.

Note, too, that there are also **quarter-note triplets**, where a half note is divided into three equal quarter-note subdivisions (3 notes over 2 beats), and **16th-note triplets**, where an eighth note is divided into three equal 16th-note subdivisions. We'll cover those later in the book.

Let's plug the A5, D5, and E5 power chords you learned in Chapter 5 into the 12-bar blues form and try playing through using the shuffle rhythm. Listen to the audio to get the feel. Once you hear it, you'll definitely know it.

Fig. 80

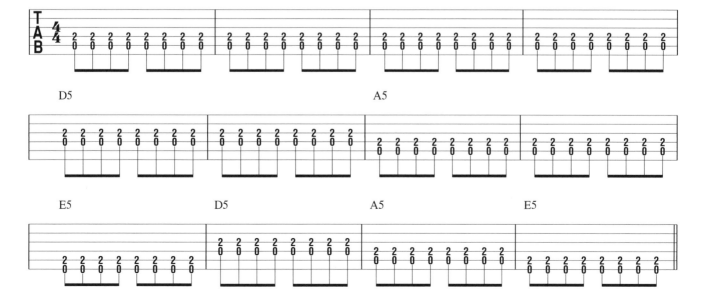

The "5–6" Boogie/Shuffle

Now the fun really begins. The **5–6** chord pattern refers to the timeless alternation of a "5" chord (power chord) and the two-note version of a "6th" chord, which contains the root and 6th degree of the chord's base scale. You've heard it in a shuffle rhythm in countless blues tunes as well as rock 'n' roll classics like Buddy Holly's "That'll Be the Day," and in a straight boogie in songs like Chuck Berry's "Johnny B. Goode," and the Beach Boys' "Fun, Fun, Fun," to name just a few.

To play the pattern using open-position chords (A5, D5, E5), simply alternate between the index-fingered chord and, while still playing the open-string root, your ring finger two frets in front of your index. For example, here are the A5 and A6 chord shapes. The same applies to D5 and D6 as well as E5 and E6, using the appropriate root notes.

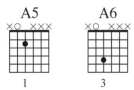

OK, let's try playing an A5–A6 shuffle pattern.

Fig. 81

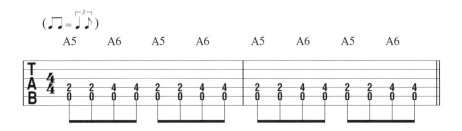

Now let's try this pattern over a full 12-bar blues form in the key of A. Note that in this example, we don't identify every change from "5" to "6," but instead just give you the chord root for each change. As you read through sheet music of your favorite blues and rock tunes that use the 5-6 shuffle, you'll find that sometimes each and every change is indicated, and sometimes you just get the basic harmony. In the latter cases, and you need to rely on the rhythm tab to know when to change. (You can also try playing it palm-muted.)

Fig. 82 🔊

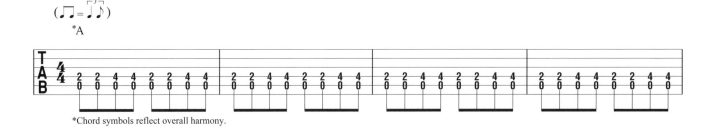

*Chord symbols reflect overall harmony.

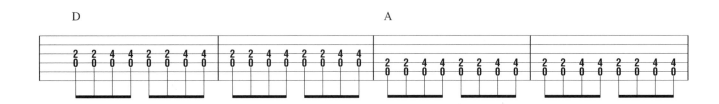

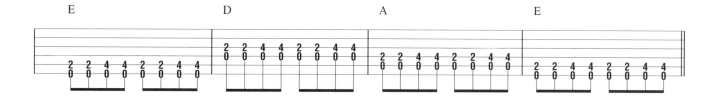

The same 5–6 shuffle can be applied to keys not in open position, too, using the movable two-note power chords you learned in Chapter 5 as your base. But this means that you need to be able to stretch your fret hand's pinky finger two frets ahead of your ring finger to hit the "6" chord. Don't worry, it's not as tough as it sounds. Here are A5 and A6 chord shapes again, this time using the movable two-note shape at the fifth fret (6th-string root).

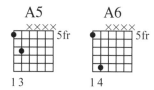

When you stretch for the "6," be sure to keep your ring finger anchored on the "5" the whole time. This habit will help immensely when playing uptempo shuffles.

To get you started, we'll play through a blues in C, using the C5 at the eighth fret (6th-string root) as the I chord, the F5 at the eighth fret (5th-string root) as the IV chord, and the G5 at the tenth fret (5th-string root) as the V chord. The farther up the neck you play, the easier it is to make that stretch. Additionally, you'll notice that you switch to the IV chord for bar 2, then return to the I for bars 3–4 and continue the 12-bar form as you already know it. This is called a **quick-change blues** and is a very popular alternative to the standard form.

Fig. 83

*Chord symbols reflect overall harmony.

The 7th Chord

In addition to the 5–6 shuffle, another definitive sound of the blues—as well as swing, old-school country, and even pop—is the **dominant 7th chord**, also known just as the **7th chord**. Like major and minor chords as well as power chords, there are open-position 7th chords and movable shapes. For now, we're going to stick with a small selection of open shapes that will allow you to play the blues in the keys of A and E—easily the two most popular blues guitar keys.

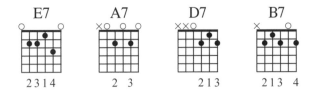

To practice these new chords, let's start with a couple of simple four-bar exercises in which you'll strum the full chords in a slow shuffle rhythm, using alternating down and up strums (Strum Pattern 2). This first one is in the key of A.

Fig. 84

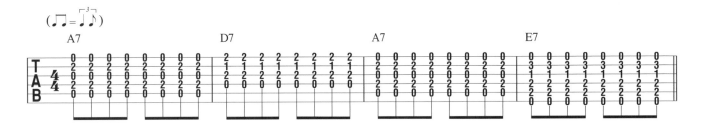

And now let's try the same thing, only in the key of E.

Fig. 85

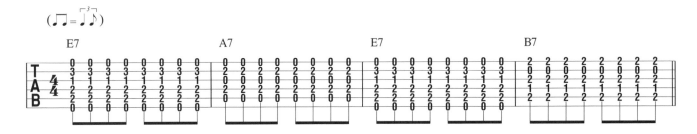

When playing the blues, you will rarely strum in a nonstop, eighth-note shuffle rhythm. This next exercise presents a very popular blues guitar shuffle rhythm based on the upbeats.

Fig. 86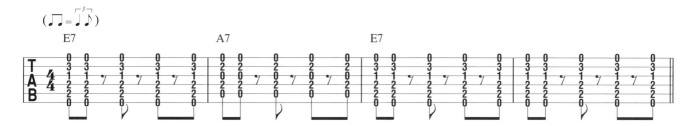

TOOLBOX

Staccato Notes

When a note or a chord is struck and then immediately stopped, it's called a **staccato** note. A staccato note is indicated with a small dot placed directly above or below the tab number, and most commonly appear as quarter notes and eighth notes.

The example below shows an E7 chord played alternately as a regular quarter note and a staccato quarter note in measure 1, then as regular and staccato eighth notes in measure 2.

Staccato Chords

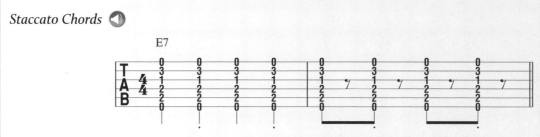

This next blues guitar rhythm is very sparse and features staccato chords.

Fig. 87

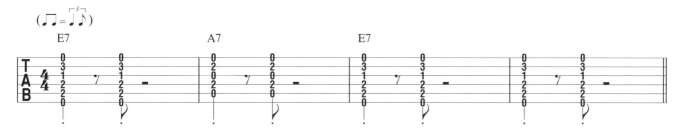

The "5–6–7" Shuffle

Another take on the 7th chord is to pair that flatted 7th degree with the root note—just like you did with the 5th and 6th—and expand the blues shuffle rhythm. Here, we'll apply it only on the open A5, D5, and E5 base chords. Whereas you used your ring finger to play the A6, D6, and E6 chords, you'll just add your pinky one fret higher to play this version of the A7, D7, and E7 chords.

Fig. 88

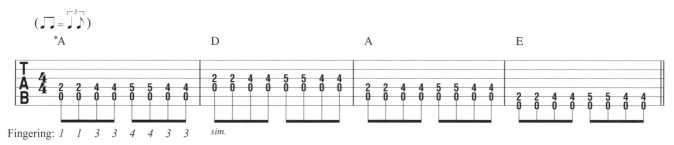

Fingering: *1   1   3   3   4   4   3   3*   *sim.*

*Chord symbols reflect overall harmony.

Jam Time

Here are a couple of famous rock 'n' roll tracks that put some of your new skills to work.

"THAT'LL BE THE DAY"
Words and Music by Jerry Allison, Norman Petty and Buddy Holly

This early rock 'n' roll shuffle is built on the 5–6 shuffle. The excerpt presented here is the song's chorus section. You may find the switch from the big E7 chord to A in the final bar a bit tricky. This is the perfect place to use your middle, ring, and pinky fingers for the fretted notes of the A chord.

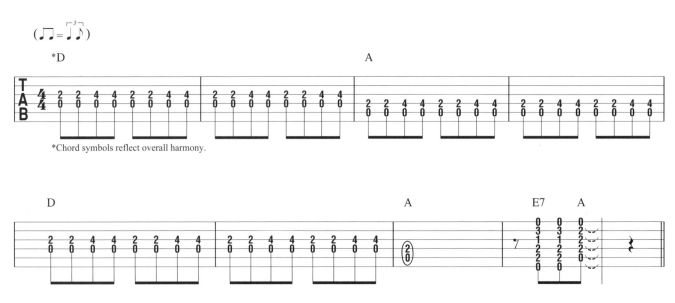

*Chord symbols reflect overall harmony.

"COME TOGETHER"
Words and Music by John Lennon and Paul McCartney

The verse to "Come Together" is neither a shuffle nor a boogie, but it is a classic use of the 5–6 rhythm pattern. Play it with a straight eighth-note feel and a slight palm mute.

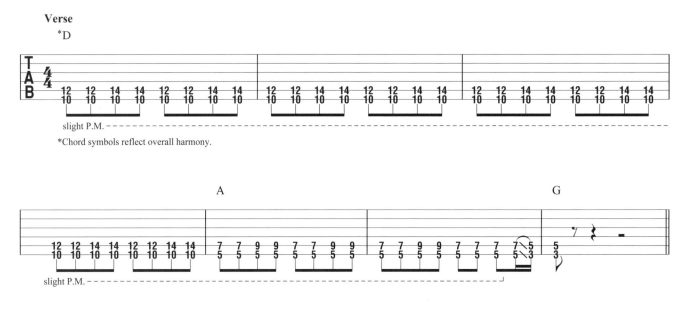

*Chord symbols reflect overall harmony.

The Turnaround

One of the most important tools in playing the blues is the *turnaround*, which occurs in bars 11–12 and serves to "turn the tune around" to set up the next 12-bar chorus. There are countless variations, and once you're a seasoned guitarist, it's best to know at least a half dozen. But for now, we're going to show you three basic ones—two in the key of E and one in the key of A.

Many of the most common turnarounds use *chromatic* movement; that is, moving a note or a pattern of notes either up or down the neck in half-step (one-fret) increments. When used, the chromatic line typically begins on beat 2 of bar 11, with the root of the I chord filling beat 1. Here's a basic one in the key of E.

Turnaround 1 in E

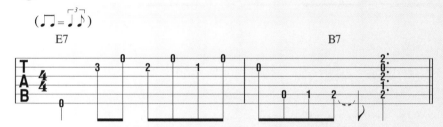

For this turnaround in E, which features an eighth-note triplet rhythm, use your fret hand's middle and ring fingers on strings 3 and 1, respectively, as indicated beneath the tab staff.

Turnaround 2 in E

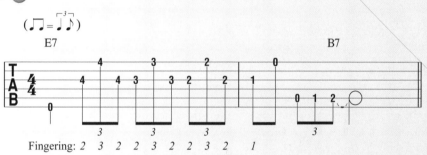

For this turnaround in the key of A, plant your pinky finger on the 1st string at the fifth fret and then follow the fingering instructions beneath the staff.

Turnaround 3 in A

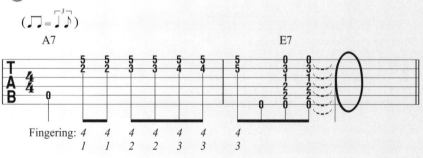

Although this all-time classic blues has been recorded and performed by myriad artists, perhaps most notably appearing in *The Blues Brothers* film, "Sweet Home Chicago" was written by the seminal Delta bluesman Robert Johnson in the 1930s. The version presented here is built on the basic, 5–6 shuffle rhythm, with an occasional 7th thrown in, and it features not only a turnaround but also an **intro**, which is just a turnaround played at the start of the tune to give it a little momentum.

"Sweet Home Chicago" appears on the next page to allow for easier reading.

"SWEET HOME CHICAGO"

Words and Music by Robert Johnson

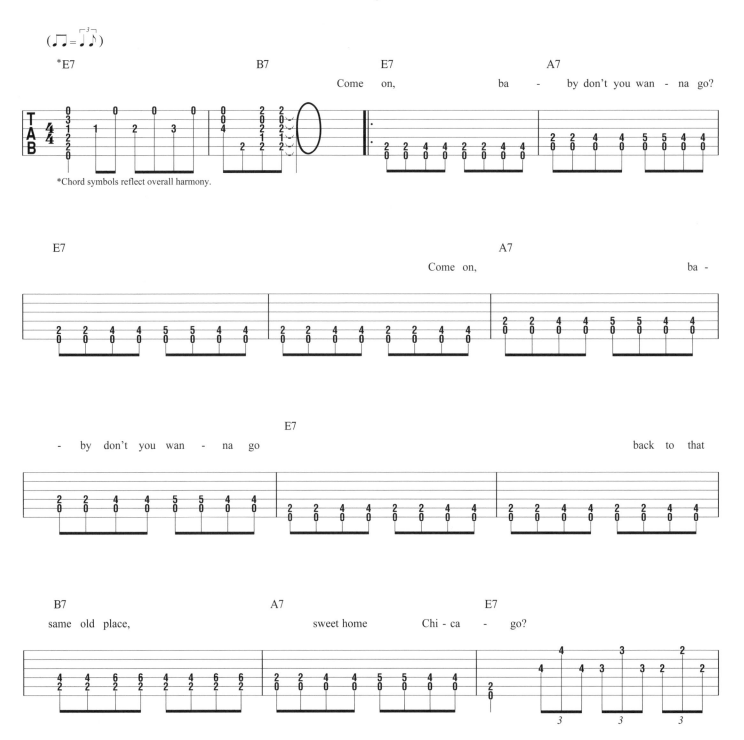

*Chord symbols reflect overall harmony.

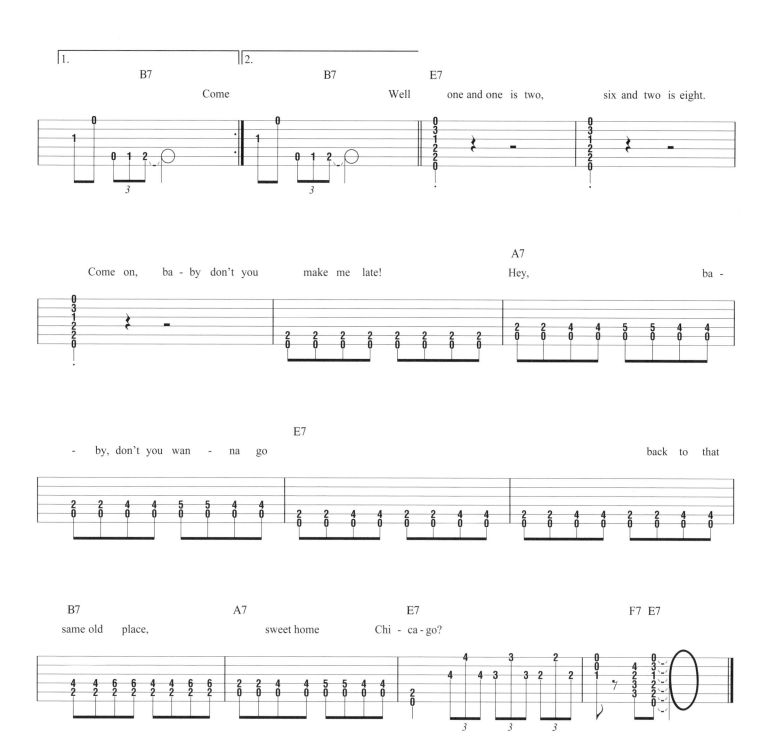

Chapter 9 ▶

Lead Techniques

In this chapter, you'll learn some of the scales and techniques used to play "lead guitar," including legato techniques, string bending, and vibrato.

Lead Guitar

In the world of electric guitar, there are two basic types of guitar players: 1) **rhythm guitarists**, who play chords and riffs that, along with the drums and bass, form the foundation of a given song (and which is what you've been learning so far); and 2) **lead guitarists**, who use various scales to play primarily single-note melodic licks, fills, and solos.

The basis for almost all scales and chords in popular music—whether it's rock, blues, country, pop, or folk—is the major scale. The major scale contains seven notes, or scale degrees, numbered 1–7, so the major scale formula is 1–2–3–4–5–6–7. If you alter (flat or sharp) or remove any of those notes, it becomes a new scale.

As critical as understanding the major scale is to becoming a complete guitar player, we're instead going to start with the most commonly used scale in popular music.

The Minor Pentatonic Scale

The **minor pentatonic scale**, which contains just five notes (**pentatonic** translates as "five notes"), is by far the most popular scale used by guitarists across popular music genres. It contains the root, ♭3rd, 4th, 5th, and ♭7th notes of the major scale, so its formula is 1–♭3–4–5–♭7. In the key of C, these notes are C–E♭–F–G–B♭.

Fig. 89 🔊

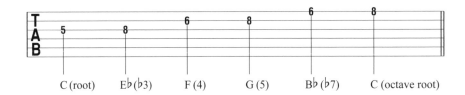

C (root)   E♭ (♭3)   F (4)   G (5)   B♭ (♭7)   C (octave root)

There are five different fingerings for the minor pentatonic scale, but the **minor pentatonic box** shape is the most common. The root note is on the 6th string, played with your index finger, so you can play the minor pentatonic scale in any key simply by moving your index finger to the key's root note.

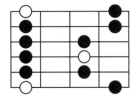

open circles indicate root notes

Here it is in fifth position, making it an A minor pentatonic scale. Practice playing it up and down the pattern, using alternate picking.

Fig. 90 🔊

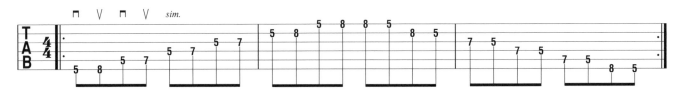

You probably played all the seventh-fret notes with your ring finger and the eighth-fret notes with your pinky finger. That's perfectly fine, but many, if not most, guitarists use their ring finger for *all* of the seventh- and eighth-fret notes, except perhaps the eighth-fret note on the 6th string. The reason for doing so is that your ring finger tends to be much stronger than your pinky, and when you start bending strings (which will be in this chapter!), you may find it helpful. So go back and play the scale again, this time using just your index and ring fingers.

Licks

Ready for your first lead guitar licks? A **lick** is a short melodic phrase that typically stands on its own and becomes a "signature" phrase. For example, you might hear the phrase, "B.B. King lick," and that would be a guitar lick made famous by B.B. King.

Your first two licks come right from the A minor pentatonic scale. Try using both your ring and pinky fingers for the eighth-fret notes and use whichever feels more comfortable to you.

Fig. 91

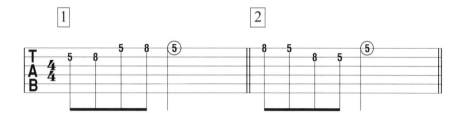

Legato Techniques: Hammer-Ons and Pull-Offs

A key tool for many musicians and especially guitarists is the **legato technique**. Literally meaning "smooth," you've already learned one legato technique—the slide—back in Chapter 5, where you applied it to power chords. You'll use legato slides even more frequently when playing lead guitar.

The two most important legato techniques for guitarists, though, are **hammer-ons** and **pull-offs**. As the name implies, a hammer-on indicates that to sound a note, you literally "hammer" a fret-hand finger down onto the fretboard to sound a note without picking it. This usually occurs after picking the previous note. In the example below, a small curved line that looks like a tie indicates that you should use a hammer-on to go from the first note to the next. Pick the notes at the fifth fret and then hammer your ring finger down onto the same string at the seventh fret to sound that note. For the hammer-ons at the eighth fret, try both your ring finger and your pinky. Don't rush it; you still need to maintain the rhythm.

Hammer-Ons

Conversely, the pull-off technique requires you to pick a note and then "pull off" your finger to sound a lower-pitched note on the same string. Be sure that you have both notes fretted prior to picking the first note, so that when you pull your finger off, the next note sounds clearly. Also, be aware that you're not simply *lifting* your finger off the string but rather pulling the string slightly as you remove your finger—it's like a light plucking action using your fret-hand finger.

Pull-Offs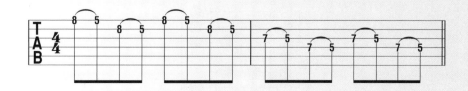

TOOLBOX

Finally, you can also combine hammer-ons and pull-offs, where you pick just the first note, then hammer onto a second note, and then pull off to a third note. Or, pick a note, pull off to a second note, and then hammer onto a third note.

Hammer-Ons and Pull-Offs Combined

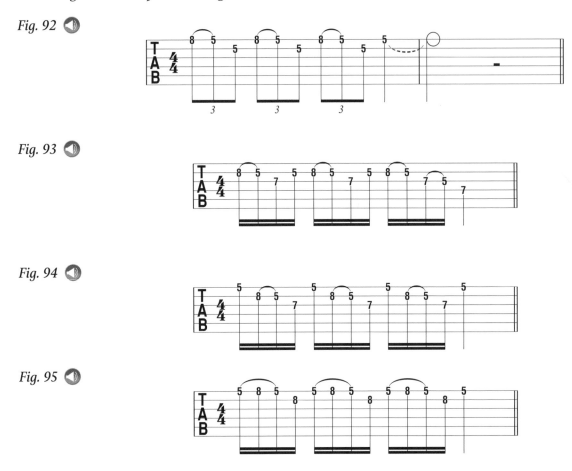

Let's take a look at some more minor pentatonic licks, incorporating legato techniques along the way. These are all considered "stock licks"; that is, these phrases have been used by countless guitarists in countless songs, thus becoming essential repertoire for guitarists.

Fig. 92

Fig. 93

Fig. 94

Fig. 95

The Blues Scale

Closely related to the minor pentatonic scale, the **blues scale** contains six notes—the same five notes of the minor pentatonic plus a flatted 5th degree: 1–♭3–4–♭5–5–♭7. So the A blues scale contains the notes A–C–D–E♭–E–G. That flat 5th (E♭), when used properly, lends a "bluesy" quality to your phrases; hence, the scale's name.

Here's a scale diagram of the blues scale box pattern.

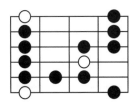

Let's play the blues scale ascending and descending in the key of A.

Fig. 96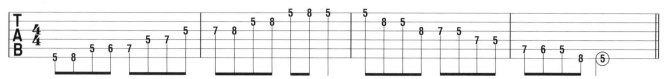

A7

Now, let's revisit Licks 2 and 3 from above, but substitute the ♭5th of the blues scale for the 4th (D) that's played in those two licks.

Here's the first variation.

Fig. 97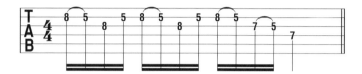

And here's a variation on Lick #3, using the ♭5th of the blues scale.

Fig. 98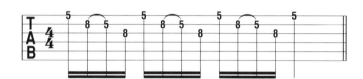

Vibrato

Ever notice how when opera singers hold a long note, their voice sort of quivers? That's called **vibrato**, and guitarists can achieve the same effect by gently shaking or wriggling a fretted note while holding it.

Though there are times when you'll want a note to ring without any vibrato, most of the time you'll use the technique. Vibrato has two elements: speed (how fast/slow you shake it) and amplitude (how far from the original pitch you push it). Finding the "sweet spot" of the vibrato technique is key—shake it too fast, and it may sound annoying; too wide, and it might make the note sound too sharp or out of tune.

Listen closely to the audio demo of the notes below to compare various types of vibrato. The first one is pretty standard, the second is slightly faster, and the last one a slow and wide vibrato.

Vibrato Technique

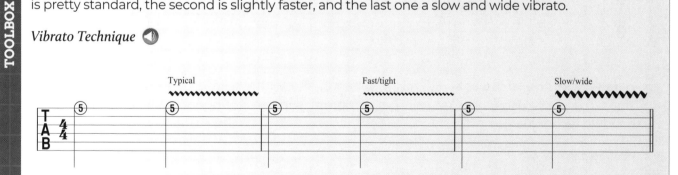

Each has its place, and that is determined both by the context of the song and by the player's individual style. Vibrato is an expressive technique and thus tends to be a fairly personal one. As you work on your own vibrato technique, be sure to practice producing it with all four fret-hand fingers.

Here's a blues-rock phrase using the A minor pentatonic scale. Be sure to apply some vibrato to the held notes.

Fig. 99

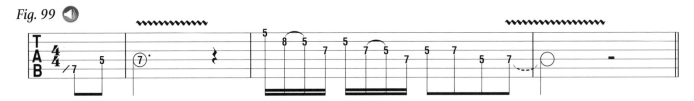

This next phrase, from the G minor pentatonic scale, is one you could hear in a ballad of just about any musical style. For the initial pickup bar, which starts on the "and" of beat 3, begin the phrase with your fret hand's ring finger at the third fret, sliding up to the fifth, which then puts you in proper position for the entire line.

Fig. 100

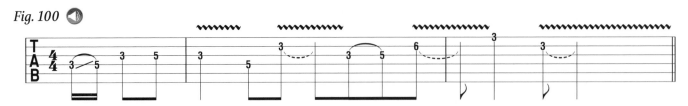

String Bending

Another critical tool for the lead guitarist is **string bending**. This highly expressive technique can help to give a musical phrase a more voice-like, or singing, quality. The technique requires you to push or pull a fretted string across the fretboard, thus raising the fretted note's pitch. The most common bends are **whole-step** and **half-step**. Bends are notated in rhythm tab with an upward-curved arrow immediately following the fretted note with the amplitude of the bend indicated by a "1" (whole-step bend) or "1/2" (half-step bend).

A key element to effective string bending is to make sure the bend is in tune. The only way to achieve this is with consistent practice and listening, but here's how to get started on the requisite ear training. First, play the note you wish to bend, then play the note you want to bend the original one up to (the **target** note). Keeping that sound in your ears, go back to the original note, pick it, and then bend the string until its pitch matches the target note. Use your ring finger to bend the string, with your index and middle fingers also down on the string behind it, helping to push the string upward, toward your head.

Whole-Step Bends

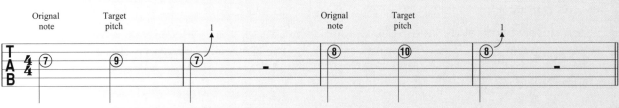

Here's the same exercise, only with half-step bends. Also, for the second bend, use your index finger alone. This is a little tougher than using your ring with supporting fingers, but it's an essential bending technique.

Half-Step Bends

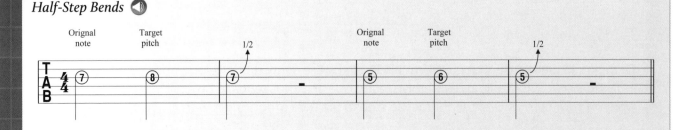

Practice both the whole- and half-step bends in this manner up and down the fretboard. You should also try both bends on the 1st string. Bends of one whole step or more typically only occur on the top three strings, but half-step bends can be found on all six strings.

*Bending Rule of Thumb: Bends on the top three strings are usually executed by pushing the string upward, toward your head. Those on the bottom three strings are done by pulling the string downward, toward the floor.

Let's try some must-know licks that include whole- and half-step bends on the top three strings.

Must-Know Bending Lick 1

This first one, typically credited to Chuck Berry, is one of the all-time must-know moves upon which many licks have been built. Place your index finger on the 2nd string at the fifth fret, and use your ring finger—aided by your middle finger—to bend the 3rd string to the target pitch, which, in this case, matches the note at the fifth fret on the 2nd string.

Fig. 101

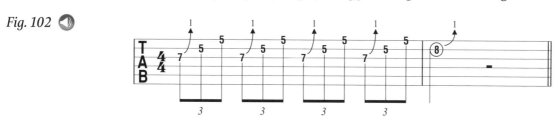

Must-Know Bending Lick 2

This one builds on the previous lick and is an even more popular phrase. Here, anchor your index finger across strings 2–1 (like when playing the F chord), and use your ring finger to produce the bend on the 3rd string. Try executing the final 8th-fret bend with your pinky finger, using your ring and middle fingers for extra support.

Fig. 102

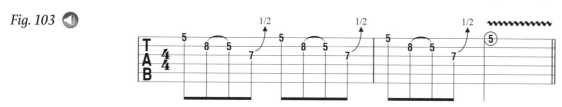

Must-Know Bending Lick 3

This next one is essentially the same as the blues scale variation on Must-Know Lick #3 you learned earlier this chapter, only it uses a half-step bend to reach the bluesy ♭5th, rather than fretting the note. Anchor your index finger across strings 2–1 and use your pinky for the eighth-fret pull-off notes, and your ring finger for the bends.

Fig. 103

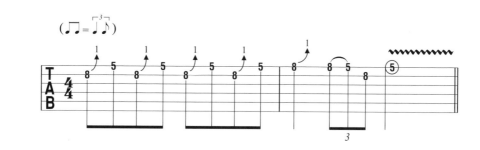

Must-Know Bending Lick 4

This one is similar to the Chuck Berry motif in Bending Lick 1 but takes place on the top two strings with no rests and adds a shuffle feel.

Fig. 104

Bend and Release (and Pull Off)

Another great tool to add to your string-bending Toolbox is the **bend-and-release** technique. Just as the name implies, this technique involves bending a string to a target pitch and then, without picking the note again, releasing the bend back to the original pitch.

Bend and Release

Building on the example above, you can also add a pull-off to the lower fretted note *after* you release the bend. So you only pick the first note over the course of beats 1–2 and 3–4.

Bend and Release with Pull-Off

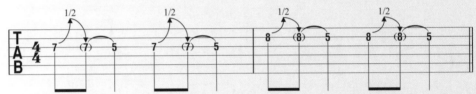

The bend-release-pull-off move using the A blues scale is frequently employed using a 16th-note triplet rhythm. If you'll recall, a triplet divides a given note into three equal subdivisions, so a 16th-note triplet is three 16th notes in the space of a single eighth note. Here's a classic lick using the bend-and-release-pull-off move in a 16th-note triplet rhythm.

Bend and Release Lick

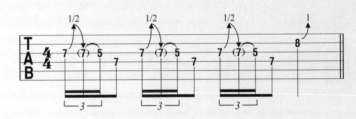

Jam Time

Here are some licks recorded by some of the greatest guitar players of all time in some of their biggest hits.

"CAN'T BUY ME LOVE"
Words and Music by John Lennon and Paul McCartney

The first four bars of this George Harrison solo feature bends with vibrato and bend-and-release moves in the C minor pentatonic box.

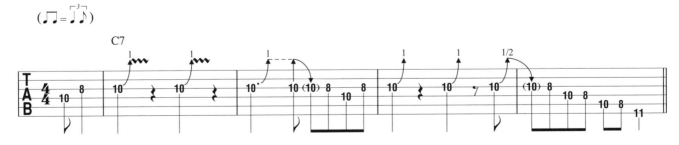

TOOLBOX

"LA GRANGE"

Words and Music by Billy F Gibbons, Dusty Hill and Frank Lee Beard

A how-how-how about this classic solo starter? After a whole-step bend kickstart, guitarist Billy Gibbons master-fully navigates a triplet-based descent through the C minor pentatonic box.

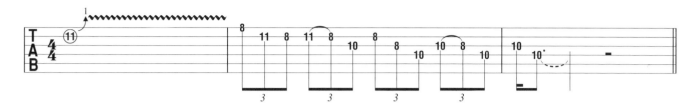

"BACK IN BLACK"

Words and Music by Angus Young, Malcolm Young and Brian Johnson

What makes this riff one of the all-time greats is the combination of punchy power chords, the slick descending minor pentatonic lick in open position (note that it begins on the second 16th-note subdivision), and the cool bass walk-up.

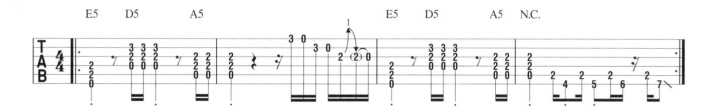

"WALK THIS WAY"

Words and Music by Steven Tyler and Joe Perry

Another of the most famous intro riffs in rock history, this one is constructed using the E blues scale in open position.

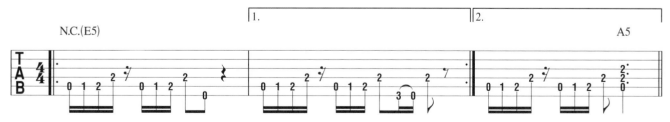

"ARE YOU GONNA GO MY WAY"

Words by Lenny Kravitz
Music by Lenny Kravitz and Craig Ross

In this throwback to Jimi Hendrix's psychedelic blues-rock sound, Lenny Kravitz put together an infectious riff built from the open-position E minor pentatonic scale. Use your fret hand's middle finger, supported by the index, to crank out those second-fret, whole-step bends.

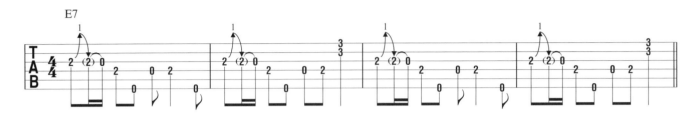

What better way to cap off a chapter on lead guitar than playing a Jimi Hendrix tune. Widely accepted as the greatest rock guitarist of all time, many of the lead guitar licks we now consider essential learning were pioneered—or at least made famous—by him.

"HEY JOE"

Words and Music by Billy Roberts

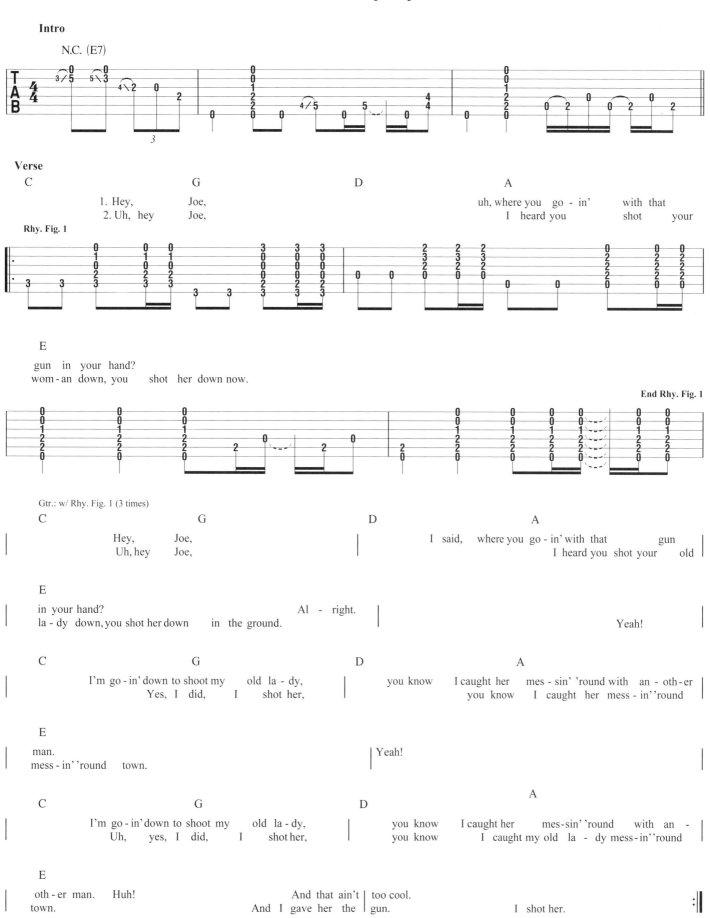

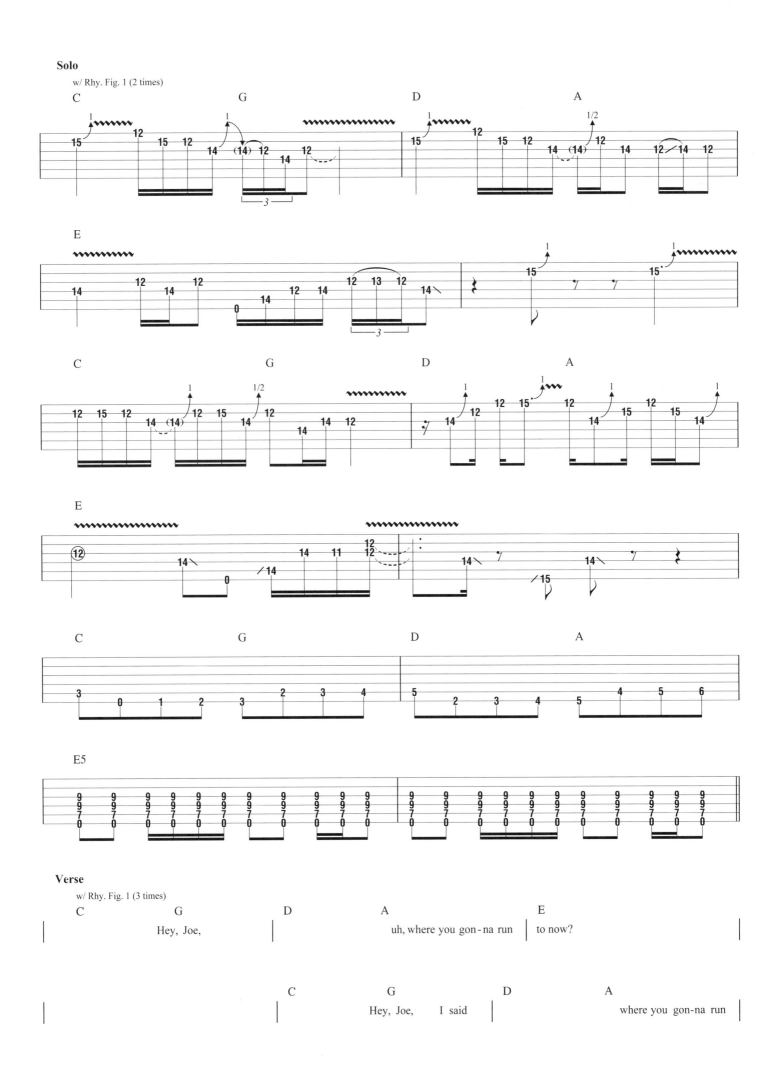

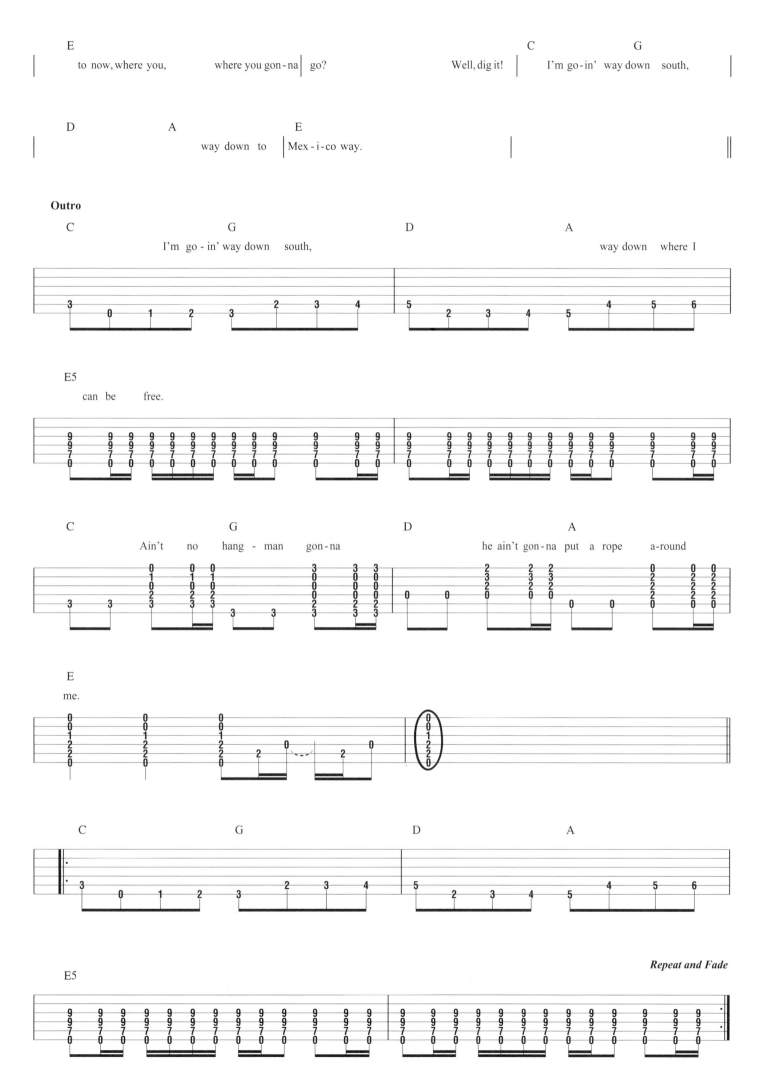

Chapter 10 ▶

Barre Chords

In this chapter, you're going to learn how to play major, minor, and dominant 7th barre chords with both 6th- and 5th-string roots.

Barre Chords

For generations of beginner guitar players, the term **barre chords** has struck fear into their hearts and hands. Sure, they take a little more elbow grease than most chords, but being able to play them is absolutely essential to becoming a guitarist.

So what is a barre chord? It's really nothing more than an open-position chord, but with your fret hand's index finger serving as the nut, representing the "open" strings of the chord. Of course, since your index finger is serving in that function, it can't be used to fret any of the other chord tones, which necessitates a re-fingering of the open chord shapes you already know.

6th-String Root—Major and Minor

The major, minor, and dominant 7th barre chords you'll learn here and use the most often in music have their root notes on either the 6th or 5th string. Let's start with the barre chord shape for major chords with a 6th-string root.

The major barre chord shape with a 6th-string root is also known as the **E-shape** barre chord, because the easiest way to show you the concept is by turning the open E major chord into a movable barre chord shape. First, fret an open E chord, *but*—use your middle, ring, and pinky fingers as shown in the chord frame below. Then, slide the whole shape up one fret and lay your index finger across all six strings very close to the first fret wire, with your thumb firmly anchored behind the neck, so that your "pinching" the neck between your index-finger barre and your thumb. Then, strum all six strings to play the F major barre chord.

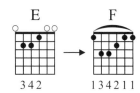

If you got all six strings to ring clearly, wow—you're a natural. In the more likely event that you encountered some muted notes, don't worry, you're in good company. Try it again, playing one note at a time, to determine which notes are muted and slightly adjust your fret-hand fingers until you can get them all to ring clearly. This will take some time and repetition, but it's so worth the effort.

The exercise below switches from F major to G major barre chords in a simple quarter-note strum rhythm. Focus on getting consistently clean strums.

Fig. 105 🔊

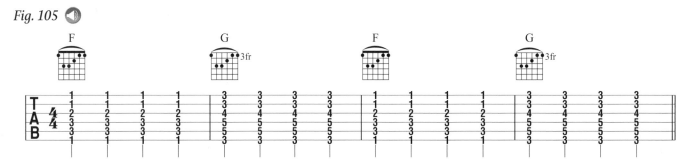

Let's try a I–IV–V progression in F using this new barre chord. This one requires you to slide the shape a little greater distance around the neck. When doing so, maintain the chord shape with your fret hand, lifting your fingers just barely enough off the frets to move your hand without sounding any notes.

Fig. 106

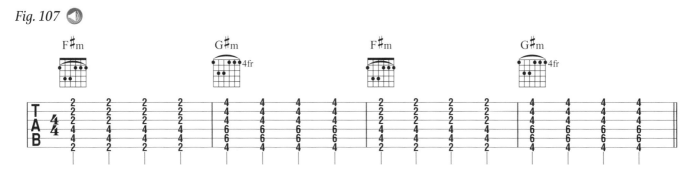

Now let's try the minor barre chord shape with a 6th-string root. Like the E-shape major, the minor is sometimes called the **Em-shape** barre chord. Here, we'll use the open Em chord as our starting point, only instead of using your middle and ring fingers to fret the chord, you'll place your ring finger on the 5th string and your pinky finger on the 4th string. Next, slide them up one fret, to the third fret, and lay your index finger across all six strings.

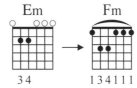

As with the major barre chord, work to make sure all six strings sound clearly. This one may be a little trickier, given that your index finger is now responsible for four of the six notes, but it will come with practice.

Let's try an F♯m to G♯m progression in a quarter-note rhythm to practice this new chord shape.

Fig. 107

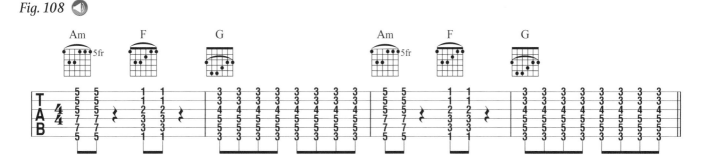

Now let's mix some major and minor chords in some standard progressions. This first one is a rock progression featuring Am, F, and G barre chords.

Fig. 108

Here's a progression in the key of G that includes some 16th-note strums offset by staccato quarter notes for a mid-1990s pop sound.

Fig. 109 🔊

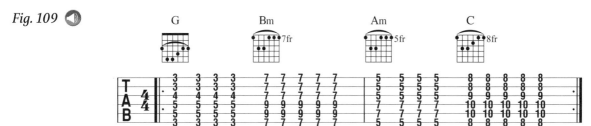

Scratch Strums

An incredibly useful tool for rhythm guitarists is the muted strum, or **scratch strum**, which produces a percussive "scratch" sound when executed properly. Represented in the rhythm tab by the "x" symbol on the string, you can produce scratch strums while playing barre chords simply by lifting all your fingers just enough so that the strings are no longer in contact with the metal fret wires, but are still in touch with your fingers, thus muting the notes. When playing open chords, however, you'll need to use a complete palm mute, where you rest your picking hand across all indicated strings just prior to strumming them, to produce the effect.

Scratch Strums 🔊

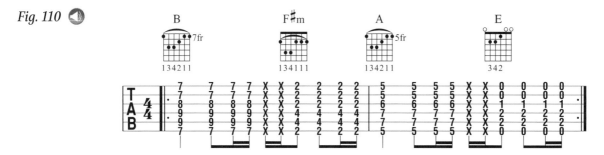

Here's a popular progression that includes the scratch strum technique.

Fig. 110 🔊

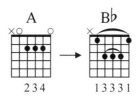

5th-String Root—Major and Minor

Whereas the 6th-string root major and minor barre chords are based on the open E and Em chords, the 5th-string root major and minor barre chords come from the open A and Am chords. As a result, you'll often hear them referred to as **A-shape** and **Am-shape** barre chords. Let's first take a look at the major chord.

To play a 5th-string root major barre chord, you actually have to form *two* barres—one with your index finger across strings 5–1, and one with your ring finger across strings 4–2. (String 6 is not played.) Here's the shape and fingerings.

Note the fingering change between the open A major and its movable major barre chord shape. This is arguably the toughest barre chord fingering for beginner guitarists, and you should do your best to get it, but there are alternatives.

Some, though not many, guitarists maintain the fingering for the open A chord and then lay the index finger across strings 5–1 two frets behind the A shape. The more common alternative, however, is to use the ring-finger barre, but use your index finger only on the 5th string, leaving the 1st string muted or unplayed as well. Just be aware that there will be songs where you need to be able to produce that note on the 1st string, but typically, you can get away with just using the second alternative below.

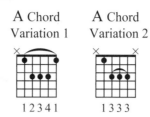

Let's give this new shape a go.

Fig. 111

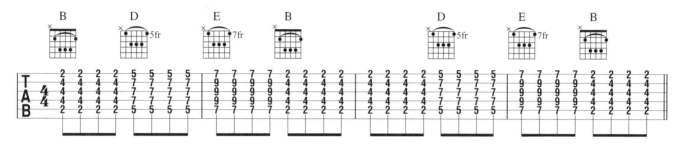

Let's try another progression using the A-shape major barre chord. This one is in the key of C.

Fig. 112

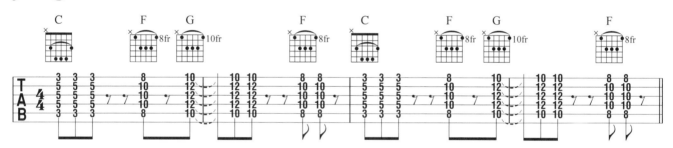

Now let's look at the 5th-string root Am-shape barre chord. For this one, simply fret the Bm chord shape you learned earlier, but this time, lay your index finger across strings 5–1, so that you include the 1st string in the chord shape. Allow your fingertip to lightly touch the 6th string so that it's muted. Just keep in mind that the Am-shape barre chord is just a movable version of the open Am chord.

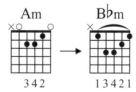

All right, let's try this new shape in an Em–Bm example.

Fig. 113

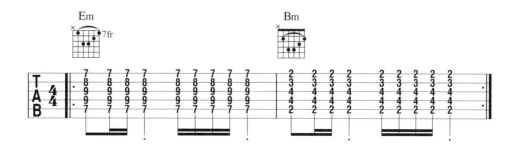

And now let's mix some major and minor 5th-string root barre chords into popular chord progressions. This first progression can be found in lots of great songs, using all sorts of different rhythms.

Fig. 114

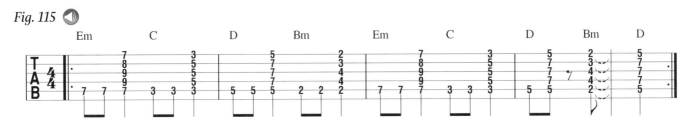

Here's one in the key of E minor, where each barre chord is preceded by playing just the root bass note. Be sure to have the barre chord entirely fretted for each bass note, and watch the rhythm in measure 4.

Fig. 115

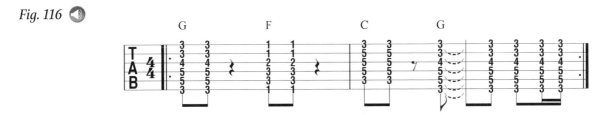

At this point, let's try a few chord progressions that include both 6th- and 5th-string rooted major and minor barre chords.

This first one uses quarter-note rests to space out the chords a bit, to help you ease into it.

Fig. 116

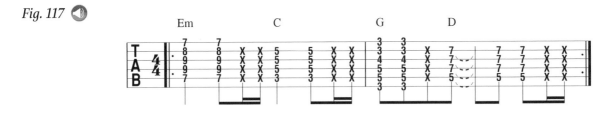

Here's another riff that uses eighth rests and scratch strums to help give you time to make the chord changes. Note, too, that the A-shape barre chords in this example use only strings 5–2.

Fig. 117

This next progression is an incredibly popular one, set here in the key of F major and in a steady, eighth-note strumming rhythm.

Fig. 118

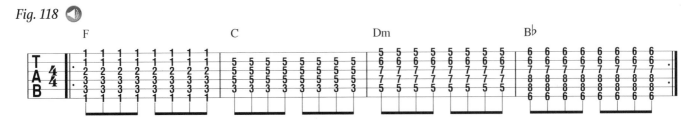

And here's a classic, blues-rock style riff that alternates between E- and A-shape major barre chords with some tasty scratch strums to add extra grit.

Fig. 119 🔊

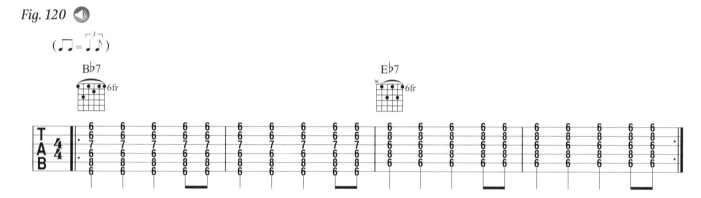

Dominant 7th Barre Chords

The final two barre chord shapes you'll learn this chapter are a 6th- and 5th-string root dominant 7th chords, based on open E7 and A7 shapes, respectively.

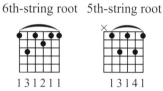

6th-string root   5th-string root

1 3 1 2 1 1   1 3 1 4 1

Here's a short exercise to help you get these shapes under your fingers. You can choose to play it swung or straight.

Fig. 120 🔊

All right, let's try a blues in the key of C using these two new 7th chord barre shapes. You can choose to play it swung or straight.

Fig. 121 🔊

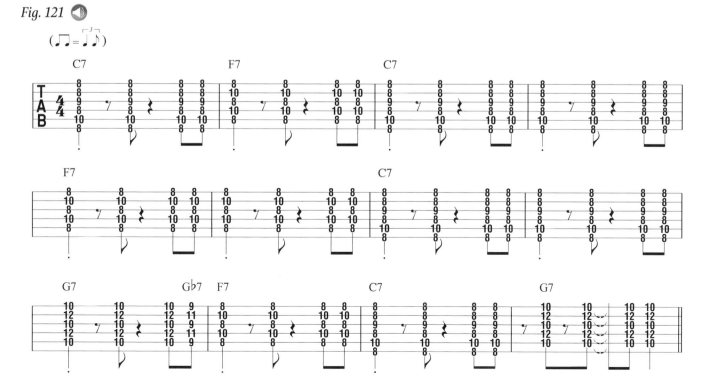

Jam Time

Let's practice all these barre chords by playing through some of the greatest chord riffs of the past 60 years.

"WALK DON'T RUN"
By Johnny Smith

This timeless instrumental has one of the most memorable melodies in the annals of surf guitar (you'll play the whole song later in this book), but the opening chords provide a terrific introduction to barre chords.

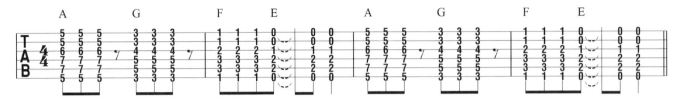

"BABA O'RILEY"
Words and Music by Peter Townshend

This early 1970s rock classic by The Who, with its long-held chords, is perfect for practicing not only barre chords but also guitarist Pete Townshend's iconic windmill strum technique (but, please, be careful, and *don't* smash your guitar when you're done).

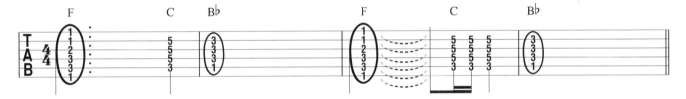

"MORE THAN A FEELING"
Words and Music by Tom Scholz

Everything that Boston recorded was "big"—big sounds, big choruses, and often, big chords. This timeless track is no exception. For the scratch strums, just lift your fret-hand fingers slightly off the Em barre chord shape to mute the strings.

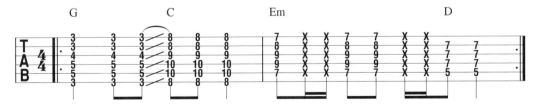

"HIT ME WITH YOUR BEST SHOT"

Words and Music by Eddie Schwartz

Guitarist Neil Giraldo crafted this powerful yet catchy riff uses only 5th-string rooted barre chords, along with an open A major chord.

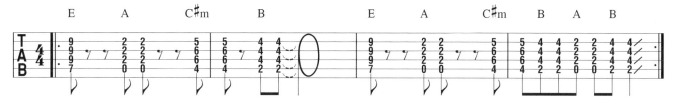

"HERE I GO AGAIN"

Words and Music by Bernie Marsden and David Coverdale

Arguably the biggest anthem to come out of the 1980s hair metal era, this tune features a huge barre chord-fueled chorus.

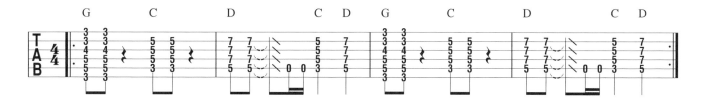

"ROLLING IN THE DEEP"

Words and Music by Adele Adkins and Paul Epworth

Though the verse of this smash hit is a terrific power-chord exercise, the chorus features some big ol' barre chords being strummed behind Adele's powerful vocals.

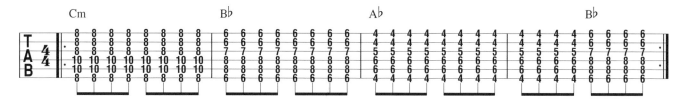

"ALL I HAVE TO DO IS DREAM"

Words and Music by Boudleaux Bryant

The chorus to this 1950s ballad is a terrific exercise in barre chords.

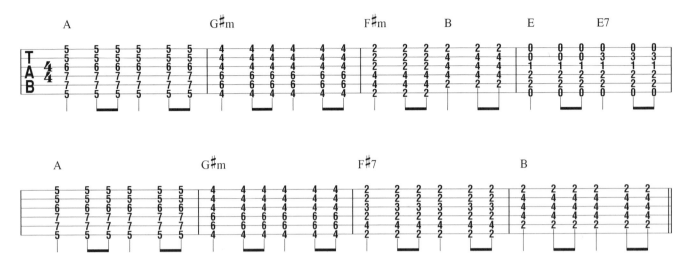

Cheat Strum

Whether you're playing open chords or barre chords, occasionally you'll come across a chord change that's really tough to make while keeping in rhythm (e.g., steady eighth-note strums at a quick tempo). When this occurs, you can almost always get away with a **cheat strum**, which is nothing more than strumming a few open strings—with a light touch—while moving your fret hand to the new chord. Here's what it sounds like. Note that you don't have to precisely strum strings 4–2 as shown below; you can just hit 4–3, or 3–2, or even 3–1 or 5–2.

Cheat Strumming

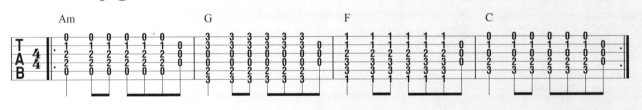

Try different variations of the G chord above.

"BODY LIKE A BACK ROAD"

Words and Music by Sam Hunt, Josh Osborne, Shane McAnally and Zach Crowell

The main rhythm guitar riff in this modern country hit features a quirky, syncopated rhythm and includes a few cheat strums, even though it's a slow-to-moderate tempo.

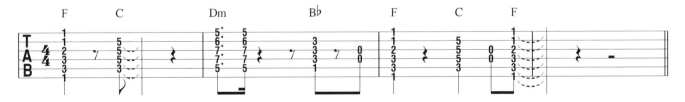

"TOES"

Words and Music by Shawn Mullins, Zac Brown, Wyatt Durrette and John Driskell Hopkins

The refrain to this summer party anthem by the Zac Brown Band comprises mostly open chords but with an F major barre chord tossed in. This is very common in pop songs set in the key of C, so you should work to become comfortable with switching to and from the F barre chord. (The asterisk in the third bar simply indicates a new chord that we haven't discussed yet, but it's super easy!)

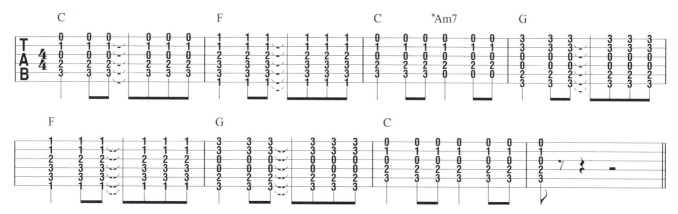

"CAN'T BUY ME LOVE"

Words and Music by John Lennon and Paul McCartney

The verse in this early smash hit by the Fab Four features C7, F7, and G7 barre chords.

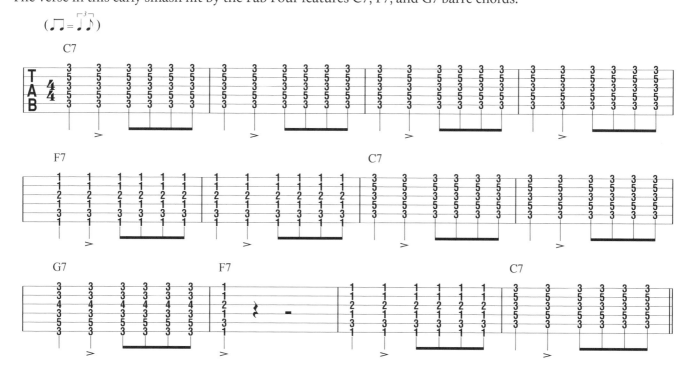

Widely considered one of the greatest pop songs of all time, Roy Orbison's "Oh, Pretty Woman" is a must-know tune for guitar players. Notice that it begins in a 6/4 time signature, which means there are six quarter-note beats in each of those measures. Later in the tune, you'll see a measure of 2/4 as well, which contains just two quarter-note beats.

"Oh, Pretty Woman" appears on the next page to allow for easier reading.

"OH, PRETTY WOMAN"

Words and Music by Roy Orbison and Bill Dees

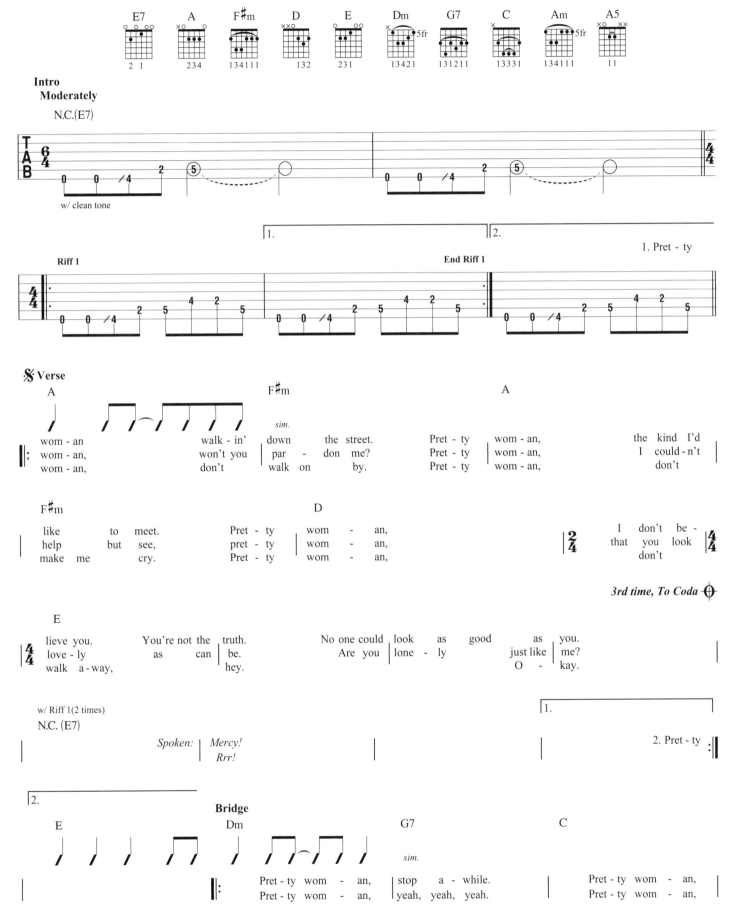

Chapter 11 ▶

Scales and More

In this chapter, you'll learn the major scale, minor scale, major pentatonic scale, some licks using these scales, and we'll expand on your string-bending techniques.

The Major Scale

Nearly all of the scales and chords that rock, pop, blues, and country guitarists use are based on the **major scale**. The major scale contains seven notes, or **scale degrees**, numbered 1 through 7 (or 8, if you include the octave of the root). There is also specific pattern with regard to the musical distance, or *interval*, between each note: W–W–H–W–W–W–H, where "W" = whole-step (2 frets), and "H" = half-step (1 fret). To help you understand the pattern, here's a C major scale all on the 2nd string.

Fig. 122

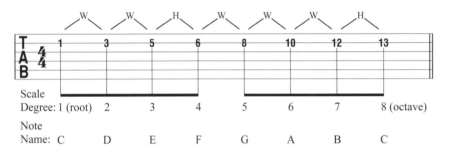

So the root of the major scale shown above is the note at the first fret on the 2nd string, or C. Following the formula, the C major scale is spelled C–D–E–F–G–A–B–(C). Although guitarists sometimes play scales along a single string, like the C major scale above, more frequently they play scales *across* several strings. For example, the scale diagram below depicts the C major scale with its root on the 6th string, at the eighth fret. Open circles represent the root (C). Anchor your index finger at the seventh fret and assign one finger per fret. Don't worry about rhythm at this point; just get a feel for fretting the notes and sounding each one cleanly.

C Major Scale—Movable Shape with Root on 6th String

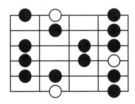

Note that you can play the above scale pattern anywhere on the neck. For example, if you want to play the A major scale, you'd simply move the entire pattern back three frets, so that the root note A is at the fifth fret on the 6th string. Here's the A major scale in tab format.

Fig. 123 ◀

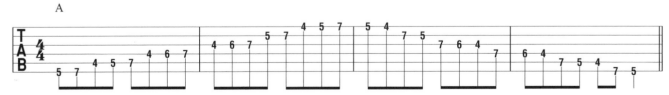

Here's a major scale pattern with its root on the 5th string and that features three notes per string, which makes it a great alternate picking workout. Note that your index finger shifts forward one fret when you get to the 3rd and 2nd strings. Strings 6–4 present quite a stretch. Most guitarists use their index, middle, and pinky fingers to play those notes, though some will substitute their ring finger for the middle.

Movable Major Scale Pattern—Three Notes Per String with Root on 5th string

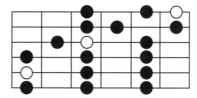

Let's try playing this pattern in E, at the seventh fret, so that the stretch isn't too uncomfortable. After you've played it a few times, shift down to the sixth fret and try the E♭ major scale, then the fifth fret for D major, and so forth, until you get all the way down to the first fret for the B♭ major scale. Remember to use alternate picking throughout the entire scale.

Fig. 124

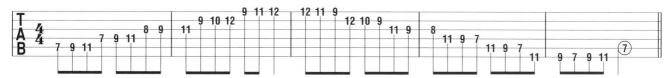

Major Scale Phrases

Let's try a few phrases built from the major scale. As opposed to the minor pentatonic scale, the major scale isn't typically used for creating "licks," but rather to build longer melodic passages. Here's a phrase you might hear in a rock ballad in the key of D major.

Fig. 125

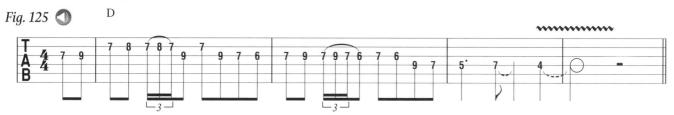

Most slow blues tunes are set in a minor key, but legendary blues guitarist B.B. King was master of the major-key slow blues as well. This B.B.-style line uses notes from the G major scale, with one extra note (C♯, ninth fret, 1st string, measure 2) that serves as a **passing tone**, which connects two scale tones and makes for a little extra pizzazz in your melody. Passing tones are most commonly heard in blues, jazz, and country guitar.

Fig. 126

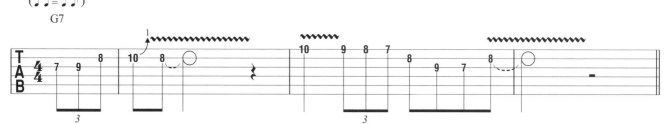

The Minor Scale

To create other scales, we simply alter, and sometimes even remove, notes from the major scale. For example, to play a **minor scale**, you flat, or lower, the 3rd, 6th, and 7th degrees of the major scale by one half-step. The resulting scale formula by number is 1–2–♭3–4–5–♭6–♭7. So, given that A major is spelled A–B–C♯–D–E–F♯–G♯, if you flat the 3rd, 6th, and 7th scale degrees, the A minor scale is spelled A–B–C–D–E–F–G.

Fig. 127

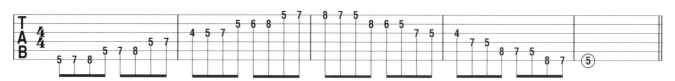

Here's a scale diagram that shows the minor scale in its movable shape with its root on the 6th string. Try playing it in every position on the fretboard.

Movable Minor Scale Pattern with Root on 6th String

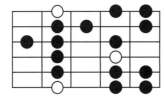

There's also a very commonly used movable minor scale shape with its root on the 5th string.

Movable Minor Scale Pattern with Root on 5th String

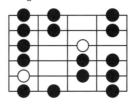

Here it is in B minor, at the second fret. Play the exercise as written, then move it up one fret and play C minor, then up again to C♯ minor, and so forth, until you reach the octave B minor scale at the 14th fret.

Fig. 128

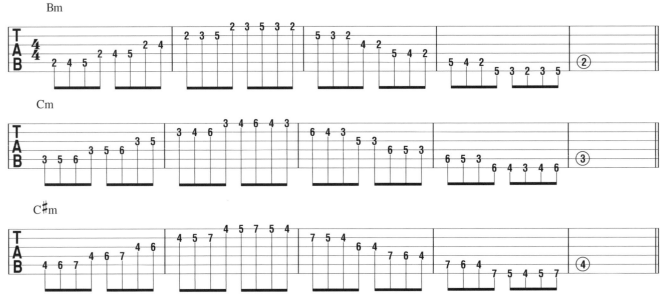

Scale Sequences

In addition to practicing your scales playing in strict ascending and descending order, you can also create patterns within the scale called **scale sequences**. For example, you can play a major or minor scale in 3rds, where you first play the root, then the 3rd degree of the scale, then the 2nd, then the 4th, then the 3rd, then the 5th, and so on. Here's what that looks like with a G major scale.

G Major Scale Sequence in 3rds

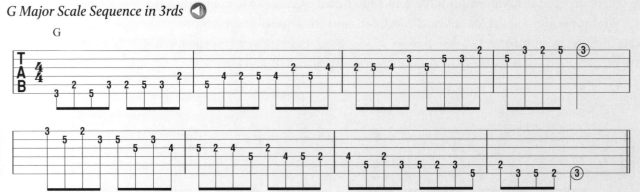

TOOLBOX

You can sequence the minor pentatonic scale, too. Here's one of the most common pentatonic scale sequences in descending order.

B Minor Scale Sequence in 4ths and 3rds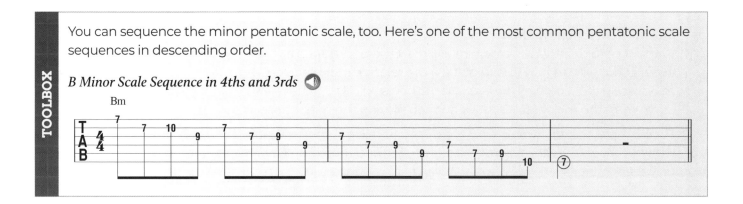

Minor Scale Phrases

Here are a couple of minor scale phrases in the hard rock style, which tends to be the domain of minor scales in soloing. The first one, an E minor line in the style of Metallica's Kirk Hammett, is constructed from the 5th-string-root, minor scale shape and features a scale sequence in an eighth-note triplet rhythm. Use your pinky, reinforced by your other fret-hand fingers, to produce the opening whole-step bend.

Fig. 129

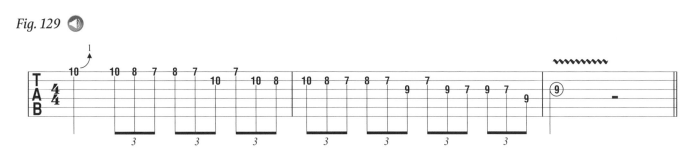

This next one, set in primarily a 16th-note rhythm, will put your legato skills to the test. It's a Randy Rhoads-style phrase in E minor, using the 6th-string-root scale pattern.

Fig. 130

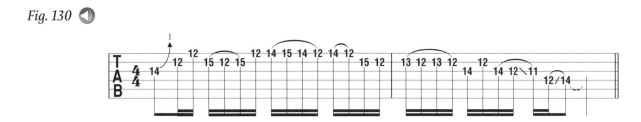

Here's a lick with a new technique and built from a linear minor scale; that is, moving up the neck along a single string, or in this case, pair of strings. The new technique is called the **unison bend**, where you bend the 3rd string up one whole step to match the fretted 2nd string two frets lower, allowing both strings to ring together. This is a great test for bending in tune.

Fig. 131

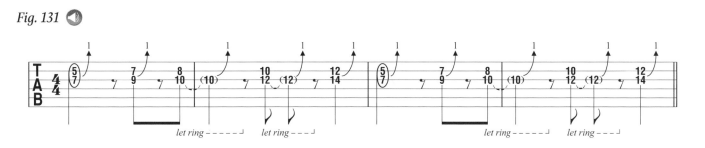

Music Theory: Relative Minor

Without getting into a full-blown music theory lesson, there's a very important concept you should know about with regard to lead guitar—the **relative minor scale**. Every major scale has a relative minor scale that contains the *exact same notes*. You'll find the relative minor by moving three frets down from the major scale's root, and then playing the minor scale shape.

For example, the relative minor of the C major scale is A minor. That is, if you play the C major scale with its root on the 6th string at the eighth fret, and then drop down three frets, to the fifth fret, and play the A minor scale, you'll find that you're playing the same notes, just starting on a different one.

C major: C–D–E–F–G–A–B
A minor: A–B–C–D–E–F–G

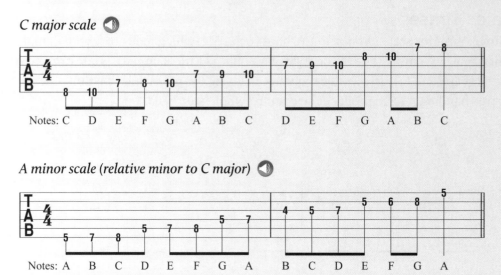

C major scale

A minor scale (relative minor to C major)

In practical terms, this knowledge is important for two purposes. First, it allows you to cover more of the fretboard when soloing. For example, if you're playing a song in the key of G major, you can use the open position E minor shape, the third-fret G major shape, the seventh-fret E minor shape, the tenth-fret G major shape, the 12th-fret E minor shape, and so on, rather than jumping between just the G major patterns you know.

Second, guitarists frequently use the relative minor scale patterns when soloing over a chord progression that is in a major key, simply because so many licks are built from minor and minor pentatonic scale shapes. For example, in the guitar solo on Queen's "Bohemian Rhapsody," which is in the key of E♭ major, guitarist Brian May uses two popular C minor scale patterns for the bulk of his lines. And in "Purple Rain," which is in the key of B♭ major, Prince used the G minor and G minor pentatonic scale patterns for much of his solo.

The Major Pentatonic Scale

One of the most widely used scales in southern rock, country, and pop music, the **major pentatonic scale** contains five notes from the major scale: 1–2–3–5–6. So in the key of C, those notes are C–D–E–G–A.

Fig. 132

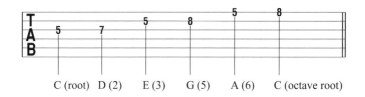

C (root) D (2) E (3) G (5) A (6) C (octave root)

Like the minor pentatonic scale, there are five scale fingering patterns, but the following two are the most common. The first includes position shifts across the fretboard.

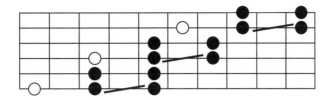

As you can see, there are three octaves of the scale shown here, each in the exact same finger pattern. You need only your index and ring fingers to play this scale, as you shift your ring finger up two frets on the 6th, 4th, and 2nd strings. When moving from the 3rd string to the 2nd, you'll need to move your index finger up one fret as well, due to the guitar's tuning.

Let's play it together in the key of G major. Note that we took it all the way up to the highest G root note (1st string, 15th fret); we did that for a particular reason, which you'll see in the example following this one. As you descend the scale, you'll use your index finger to slide back two frets where necessary.

Fig. 133

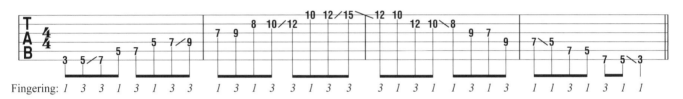

Fingering: 1 3 3 1 3 1 3 3   1 3 1 3 3 1 3 3   3 1 3 1 1 3 1 3   1 1 3 1 3 1 1

Now, let's try it again, but this time, the descent will take place entirely in 12th position.

Fig. 134

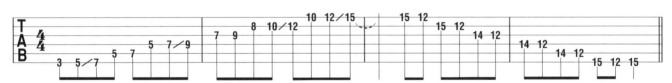

Look familiar? It should; that final descent beginning at the 15th-fret G on the 1st string matches the minor pentatonic box pattern you learned in Chapter 9. That's because E minor pentatonic is the relative minor of G major pentatonic. And just as the minor pentatonic box pattern is the most popular among guitar players, the relative major box pattern, as shown below, is the most popular major pentatonic scale pattern. You'll find it used extensively in the work of Lynyrd Skynyrd, the Allman Brothers Band, and many country artists, among others.

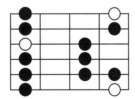

The easy way to remember the relationship here is that if you take any minor pentatonic box pattern, but instead of starting with your index finger on the 6th-string root you begin the box with your pinky finger on the 6th string, it's the same scale. In other words, A minor pentatonic is the same as C major pentatonic—same box pattern, same position (5th).

Let's try a few major pentatonic licks and phrases using both the shifting and box patterns.

This first one uses both major pentatonic patterns in conjunction with a soloing device called a **rhythmic motif**, where the notes change, but the rhythm they're played in stays consistent throughout the phrase.

Fig. 135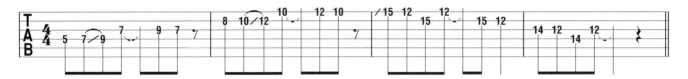

This next one is known as the "Flatt run," named for legendary bluegrass picker Lester Flatt, and is heard in countless bluegrass and country tunes. It's most commonly played in the open-position box pattern in G, with an added passing note (B♭, 5th string, first fret). (You can also slide from the B♭ to the B♮ instead of using a pull-off.)

Fig. 136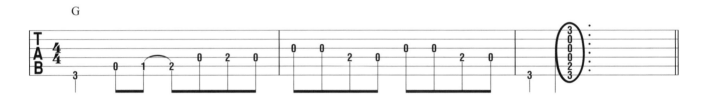

> ### Oblique Bends
>
> An essential string bending technique, the **oblique bend** is defined as bending one string while fretting a stationary note on an adjacent string. Unlike the unison bend, however, the resulting pitches do not match. Oblique bends occur most frequently when using the minor or major pentatonic box patterns, either on string set 3–2 or 2–1. Occasionally, you might hold down two strings while bending a third one.
>
> Below, you'll see some of the most commonly used oblique bends, set here in the F major pentatonic scale. Use your ring finger for the string bends and your pinky finger on the stationary notes.
>
> *Oblique Bends* 🔊

Jam Time

Let's take a look at some of the greatest riffs, licks, and solo excerpts of all time built from the major and minor scales as well as the major pentatonic.

Major Scale Songs

"JESSICA"
Words and Music by Dickey Betts

This Southern rock instrumental features an iconic main theme in A major. This isn't from a major scale fingering pattern you've learned, but rather a combination of patterns, so check out the fingering suggestions beneath the tab staff.

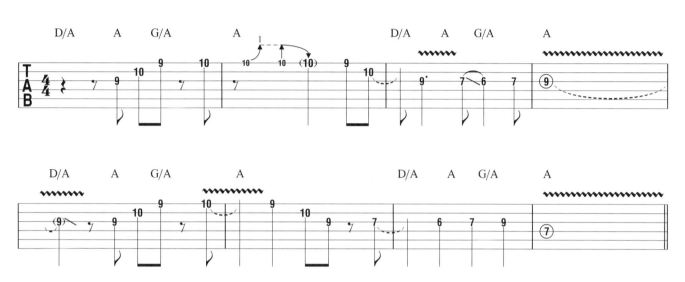

"MORE THAN A FEELING"
Words and Music by Tom Scholz

Boston guitarist Tom Scholz is also a master of the major-key solo, made no more evident than in his opening salvos in D major on this timeless classic.

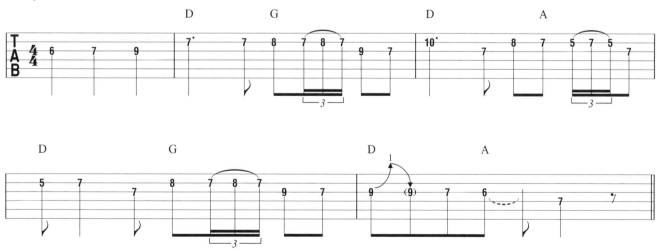

"SWEET CHILD O' MINE"

Words and Music by W. Axl Rose, Slash, Izzy Stradlin', Duff McKagan and Steven Adler

Arguably the greatest and most recognizable riff of the 30-plus years since its release, this finger-exercise-turned-iconic-riff from guitarist Slash is built from the D major scale. Careful observation tells you that only the first note every two measures changes. Place your fret hand's index finger at the 12th fret and assign one finger per fret for the most efficient fingering, with your pinky pulling double duty on the 1st string at the 15th and 14th frets. As for your picking hand, try the suggested picking directions.

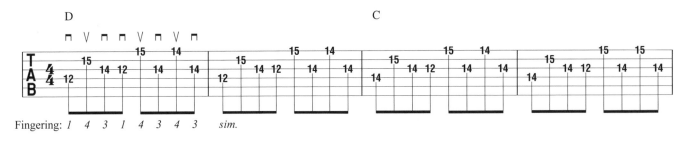

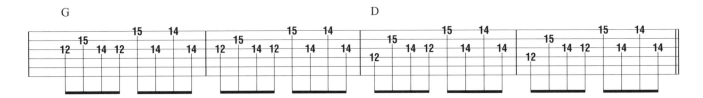

Minor Scale Songs

"LAYLA"

Words and Music by Eric Clapton and Jim Gordon

The great Eric Clapton crafted one of the most recognizable licks/riffs of all time with this gem based on the D minor scale. Notice that he jumps up to 12th position in the second half. Use your ring finger for that 15th-fret bend, ring finger for the following 12th-fret note on the 1st string, and middle finger on the 2nd string at the 13th fret, then quickly shift back to 10th position to repeat the opening legato phrase.

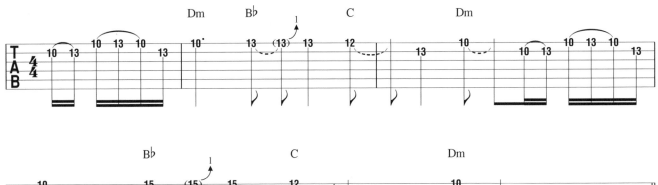

"REFUGEE"
Words and Music by Tom Petty and Mike Campbell

Guitarist Mike Campbell is one of the tastiest pickers in rock history. His intro solo in "Refugee" using the F# minor scale is a prime example.

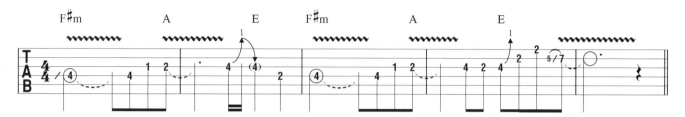

"SULTANS OF SWING"
Words and Music by Mark Knopfler

"Sultans of Swing" is widely recognized as one of the greatest guitar songs of all time, typically ranking in the top five solos in lists compiled by various guitar and music publications. Mark Knopfler's tasty four-bar intro solo using the D minor scale is the perfect aperitif to whet your whistle.

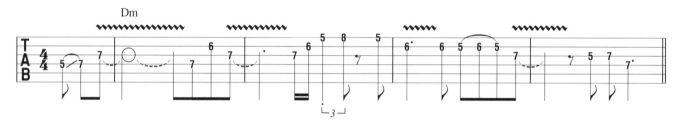

Major Pentatonic Scale Songs

"MY GIRL"
Words and Music by Smokey Robinson and Ronald White

This instantly recognizable riff is nothing but a casual stroll up one octave of the major pentatonic scale. The intro is C major pentatonic, but we included the verse here, which alternates between C and F.

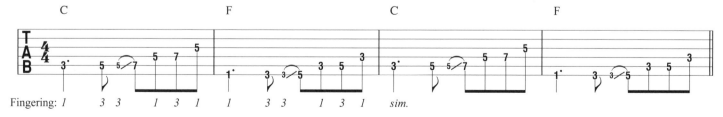

"BIRTHDAY"
Words and Music by John Lennon and Paul McCartney

Here's another based on the major pentatonic scale but with an added bluesy tone via the half-step bend at the seventh fret of the 2nd string.

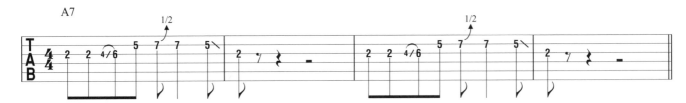

"ROSANNA"
Words and Music by David Paich

Guitarist Steve Lukather kicks off his stellar solo in the smash hit "Rosanna" with a phrase ripped from the F major pentatonic scale.

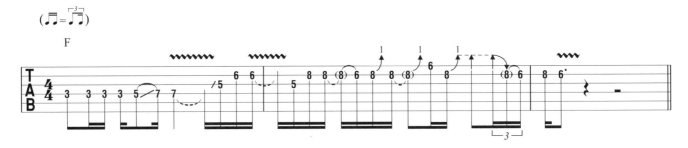

"GIMME THREE STEPS"
Words and Music by Allen Collins and Ronnie Van Zant

Here's a punchy Southern rock riff from Lynyrd Skynyrd that uses oblique bends and **double stops**—or two notes played simultaneously—pulled from the D major pentatonic box pattern at the seventh fret.

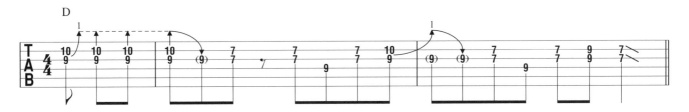

This classic surf instrumental is a like a beach-body workout for the A minor scale in open position. When the Ventures recorded it, the guitarist used a **whammy bar** on the guitar to produce some of the vibrato effects. It's a metal arm that attaches to your guitar's bridge so that when you press down on the arm, all six strings slacken, thus dropping pitch. If you press down just slightly and return it to resting position in a somewhat rapid and repeating manner, you'll get the vibrato effect. If your guitar doesn't have a whammy bar, you can use the finger vibrato you learned earlier, and if it's on an open-string note, just skip the vibrato altogether.

"Walk Don't Run" appears on the next page to allow for easier reading.

"WALK DON'T RUN"

By Johnny Smith

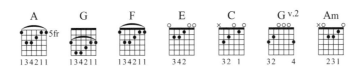

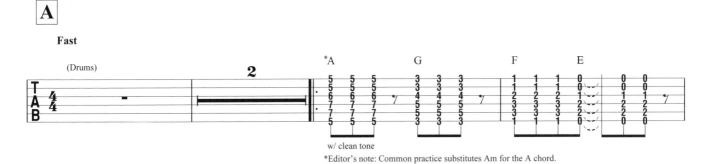

w/ clean tone

*Editor's note: Common practice substitutes Am for the A chord.

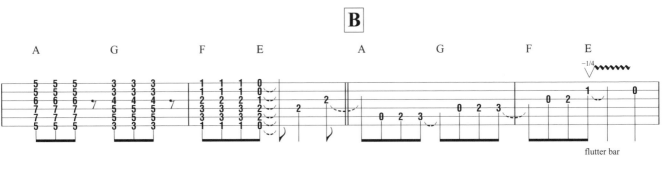

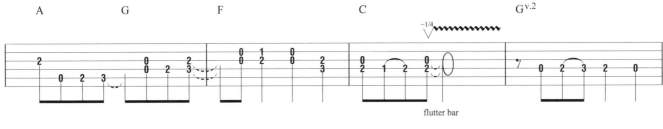

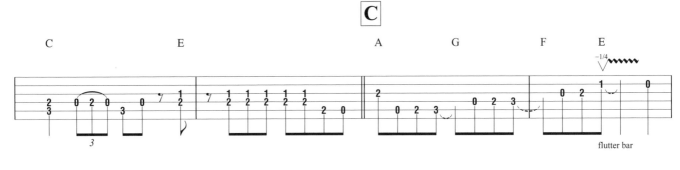

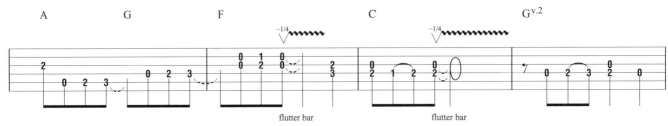

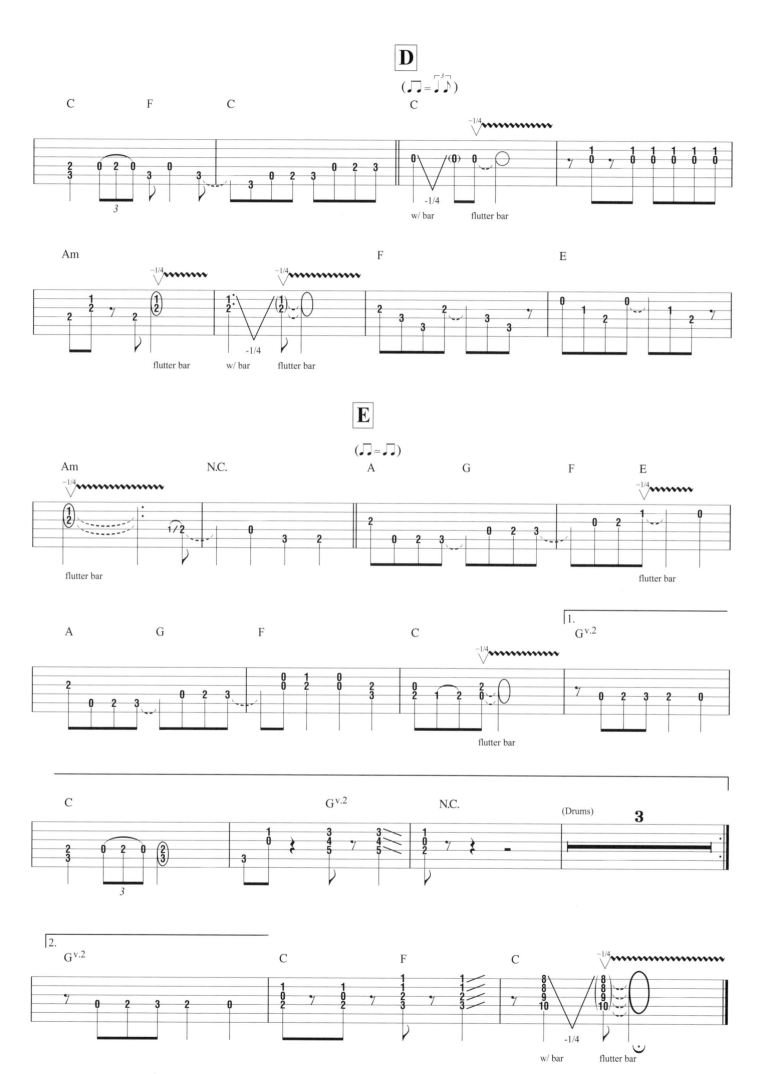

Chapter 12

Sus/Add Chords

In this chapter, you'll learn how to play "add" and "sus" chords as well as a new way to play a couple of chords that you already know.

"Sus" Chords

You've learned that major chords contain the root, 3rd, and 5th degrees of its associated major scale (e.g., C major = C–E–G), and that minor chords contain the root, ♭3rd, and 5th degrees of the same root scale (e.g., C minor = C–E♭–G). But what if a chord doesn't contain a 3rd degree but rather a 2nd or 4th?

Suspended chords, or "sus" chords, for short, are so called because they sound neither major nor minor on their own, because they do not contain a 3rd degree. The two types of "sus" chords are the suspended 2nd (sus2) and suspended 4th (sus4).

The sus2 chord contains the root, the 2nd, and the 5th; for example, the Dsus2 chord is spelled D–E–A. The sus4 chord contains the root, 4th, and 5th, so a Dsus4 chord is spelled D–G–A.

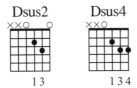

The Dsus2 and Dsus4 chords are probably the two most commonly used suspended chords in pop music. Though they can be used in isolation in place of a D major chord—particularly the Dsus2 chord—they're often used together in chord riffs like this one.

Fig. 137

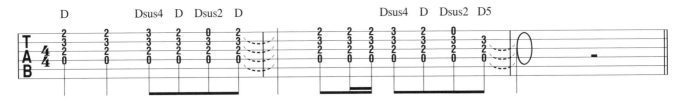

Likewise, you can do the same thing using the A major chord as your base. Here are the Asus2 and Asus4 shapes.

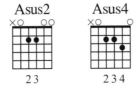

Here's that same chord riff from above, but in the key of A.

Fig. 138

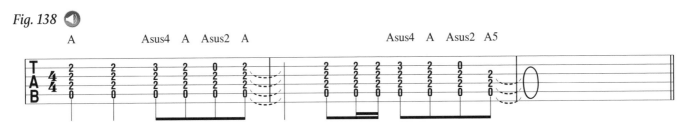

As you may have guessed, these shapes are also movable. Unlike barre chords based on the E shape and A shape, the movable sus chords are most frequently based on the A shape, and in less common but no less impactful musical instances, the D shape.

The movable D-shape sus4 chord is exactly the same as the open-position shape, except you play only strings 3–1. The movable, D-shape sus2 chord requires a small shift in fingering.

Movable D-Shape Chords

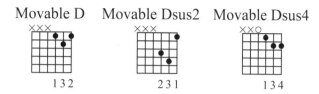

Here's a 1970s classic rock–style chord riff you might encounter using these movable D shape chords.

Fig. 139

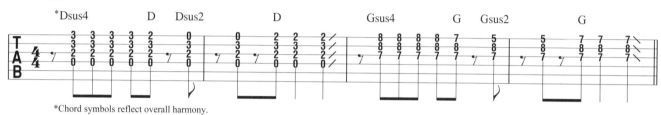

*Chord symbols reflect overall harmony.

Movable A-Shape Sus Chords

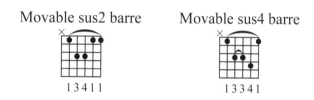

OK, let's give these a go, beginning with the movable sus2 shape.

Fig. 140

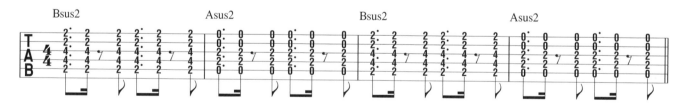

This example includes the common idea of pitting the movable sus4 chord against its associated major chord with a pedal tone—here, the chord root E—in between.

Fig. 141

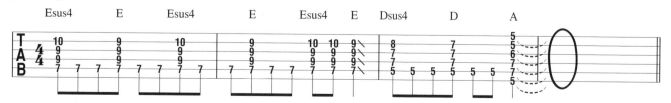

121

Add Chords

Unlike "sus" chords, **add chords** contain the 3rd degree, and still "add" another scale degree—typically the 9th (same note as the 2nd, only an octave higher) or the 4th.

Here are the most common add9 chords. Note that there are two Cadd9 chords; which one to use is usually left to the musical context such as which chord immediately precedes or follows it, but the one on the left is more commonly used.

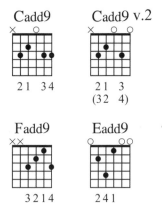

Let's try these in some basic chord progressions. The first one includes both Cadd9 versions along with the Fadd9. And since you haven't played in a shuffle rhythm in a while, you'll get that, too.

Fig. 142

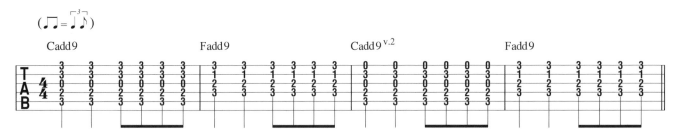

Next up is an Eadd9–Asus2 progression. Switching to that Eadd9 from the Asus2 in measure 3 will likely take some extra practice to get that pinky finger to stretch all the way to the fourth fret without touching any other strings. Make sure your fret hand's thumb is all the way behind the neck to allow for good finger arch.

Fig. 143

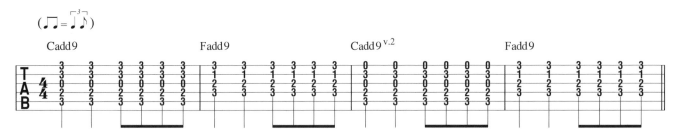

Here's the Cadd9 chord in one of its typical settings, particularly in the modern rock/pop sounds of the 1990s and 2000s.

Fig. 144

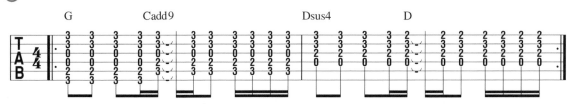

Now let's revisit that Eadd9–Asus2 progression, but we're going to toss in some arpeggio action to give the riff a little more life and some added challenge for you.

Fig. 145

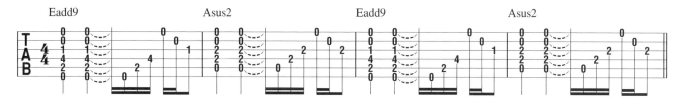

Jam Time

Let's try some of these "add" and "sus" chords out as they appear in some all-time classic songs.

"3 AM"
Lyrics by Rob Thomas
Music by Rob Thomas, Brian Yale, John Leslie Goff and John Joseph Stanley

The G–Cadd9 move is incredibly prevalent in modern pop-rock as well as modern country, as it provides both an exciting and "blank" palette over which to lay down great vocal hooks and melodies. Few have done that well as Rob Thomas and Matchbox Twenty with this 1997 smash hit. Here's the chorus.

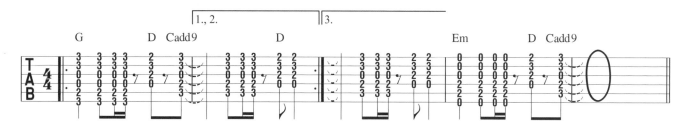

"EVERY ROSE HAS ITS THORN"
Words and Music by Bobby Dall, C.C. Deville, Bret Michaels and Rikki Rockett

Bands of the hair metal scene were using the G–Cadd9 move, along with various "sus" chords even before the alternative rock and pop bands of the 1990s. One of the tunes that has stood the test of time is Poison's monster power ballad "Every Rose Has Its Thorn." Its chorus is shown here.

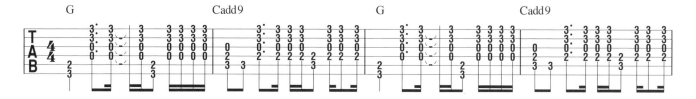

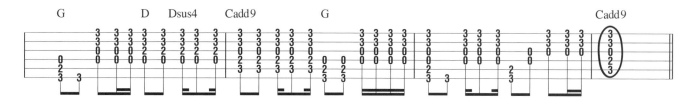

Partial Strums

As you surely noticed in the chorus excerpt of "Every Rose Has Its Thorn," there will be times—quite frequently, actually—where instead of strumming an entire chord on every beat subdivision, you will instead want or need to use a technique called **partial strumming**.

At first, it may seem intimidating trying to play just the bottom two strings, or just three middle strings, or any other partial combination while strumming along—particularly at faster tempos. But the beauty of it is that this technique not only breaks up potential monotony and lends itself to greater rhythmic effect but also is not an exact science. That's right—with very few exceptions, the choice of exactly which strings to hit when using the partial strumming technique is more of a general "I want some bass notes here, some middle notes there, and maybe a bunch of high notes in this part" decision.

So don't sweat it. If you're playing an open G major chord, and you see a transcription where you're only supposed to play strings 6–5, but you accidentally hit string 4, too, it's no big deal. Or if you're supposed to strum strings 3–1 in a 16th-note rhythm for one beat, but you actually strum strings 4–1, you're still good. That being said, if you strum strings 6–4 instead of 3–1, it probably won't sound right, so keep it in the ballpark.

"WANTED DEAD OR ALIVE"
Words and Music by Jon Bon Jovi and Richie Sambora

Another hair metal hit that has stood the test of time, "Wanted Dead or Alive" switches gears and gives you the Cadd9–G move along with cool legato play to connect the D, Dsus2, and Dsus4 chords, *and* it tosses the F major barre chord in on a pretty quick chord change just to really make you work for it. This is the verse.

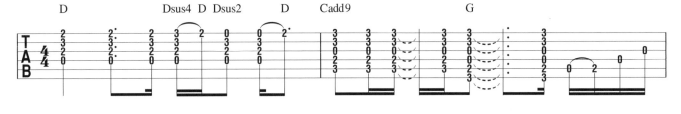

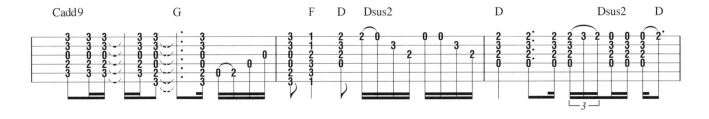

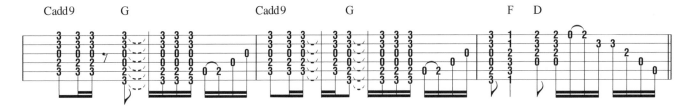

"LIGHTNING CRASHES"

Words and Music by Edward Kowalczyk, Chad Taylor, Patrick Dahlheimer and Chad Gracey

This 1994 hit by Live features the beautiful use of a sus2 chord in the verse riff. Remember how to play the scratch strums?

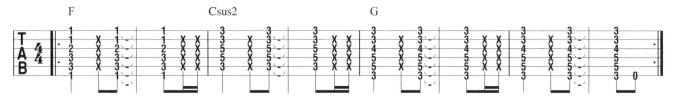

"WONDERWALL"

Words and Music by Noel Gallagher

The main chord riff in this 1995 smash by Oasis uses some sneaky syncopation combined with chord voicings that maintain the D and G notes on strings 2–1 (third fret) at all times. Keep your pinky on string 1 at the third fret and your ring finger on string 2 and the third fret at all times—do not lift them to make the chord changes. As for the chords themselves, you're probably thinking, "But I haven't learned Em7 or A7sus4 yet." Think of them this way: Em7 is the same fingering as G major, except you move your middle finger from string 6 (third fret) to string 4 (second fret); and A7sus4 is the same fingering as Cadd9, except you lift your middle finger off the 5th string (third fret) to let it ring open, leaving all others in place.

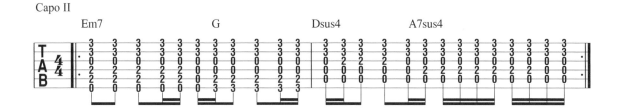

"SUMMER OF '69"

Words and Music by Bryan Adams and Jim Vallance

The interlude of this monster hit features arpeggios riding waves of Dsus2, D, and Dsus4 chords for two measures followed by Asus2, A, and Asus4 chords for two measures.

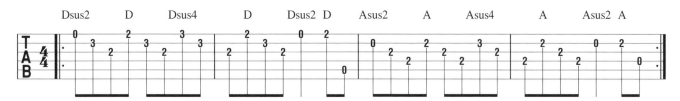

"MESSAGE IN A BOTTLE"
Music and Lyrics by Sting

Your final song riff in this section is built entirely on sus2 chords in arpeggio form. This gem from guitarist Andy Summers is a little tougher than it appears at first, but once your fingers get used to the pattern, it will fall into place rather quickly. Use your index, ring, and pinky fingers for each three-note sus2 chord shape, performing that final slide in measures 2 and 4 with your pinky finger.

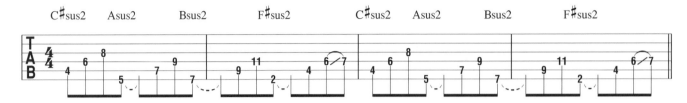

The "Keef Chords"

One of the most important chord changes in pop, rock, blues, and country music is the I–IV chord change: A–D, G–C, D–G, C–F, and more. And one of the most common ways to perform that chord change—particularly in classic rock music and *especially* in Rolling Stones songs—is what we like to call the **Keef chords**, so named for Stones guitarist Keith Richards.

Whether it's I–IV or IV–I, Keith Richards has made a career of this simple chord change, as heard in songs like "Start Me Up" and "Brown Sugar." But he's not the only one. You'll hear it in Free's "All Right Now," Boston's "Don't Look Back," Queen's "We Will Rock You," and KISS's "Rock and Roll All Nite," among many others.

Here are these two essential chord shapes. The first (the I chord) is just an open A chord shape, with all three fretted notes played with your index finger in barre format. For the second (the IV chord), maintain that A chord barre shape and place your middle finger on the 2nd string at the third fret and your ring finger on the 4th string at the fourth fret, to create a three-string D chord (D/F♯, to be precise).

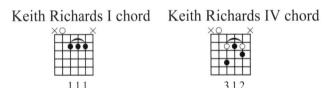

Let's try a simple riff that uses this chord move in typical rock fashion.

Fig. 146

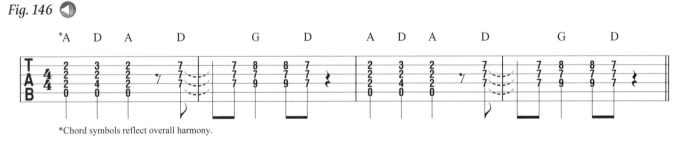

*Chord symbols reflect overall harmony.

Here's a variation where the chord riff starts with the IV-chord shape.

Fig. 147

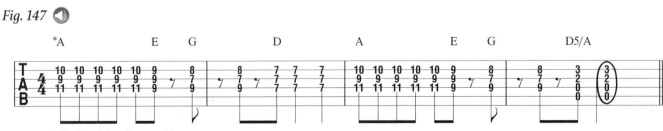

*Chord symbols reflect overall harmony.

Jam Time

Now let's take a look at some of those songs listed earlier that use these two chord shapes to such great effect.

"START ME UP"
Words and Music by Mick Jagger and Keith Richards

The Rolling Stones are responsible for several iconic rock 'n' roll guitar riffs, and this is most certainly one of them. The main reason Keith Richards became known for this particular I–IV chord move is because he uses open G tuning on his guitar and uses only strings 5–1. But open G tuning and standard tuning are the same on strings 4–2, thus allowing players in standard tuning to play the same riffs, just without the bass note that Richards gets by using open G.

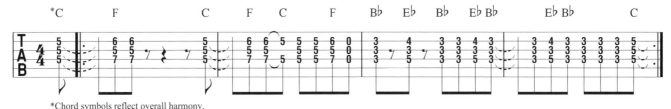

*Chord symbols reflect overall harmony.

"BROWN SUGAR"
Words and Music by Mick Jagger and Keith Richards

Equally if not more iconic than "Start Me Up," this one also is originally played in open G tuning, but again, you can cop the riff using strings 4–2, like this.

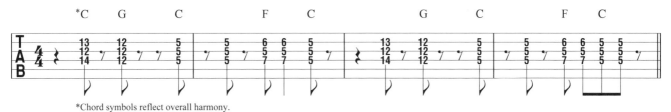

*Chord symbols reflect overall harmony.

"DON'T LOOK BACK"
Words and Music by Tom Scholz

Tom Scholz's intro riff to this classic is instant excitement with the A–D change occurring an octave higher up at the 14th fret and the adrenaline rush of the 16th-note scratch strums. Lay your index, middle, and ring fingers across all six strings to execute those muted strums while simultaneously shifting your fret hand back to seventh position for the D chord that starts the next measure.

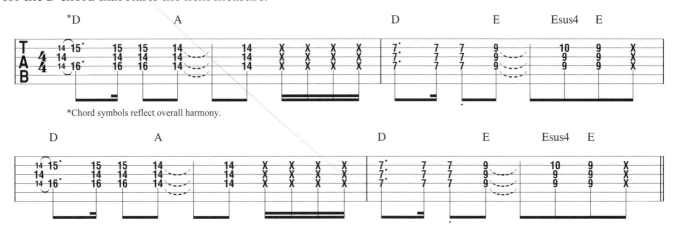

*Chord symbols reflect overall harmony.

"NOTHIN' BUT A GOOD TIME"
Words and Music by Bobby Dall, C.C. Deville, Bret Michaels and Rikki Rockett

The intro riff to this hair metal party anthem features the I–IV move in A, but up a full octave at the 14th fret.

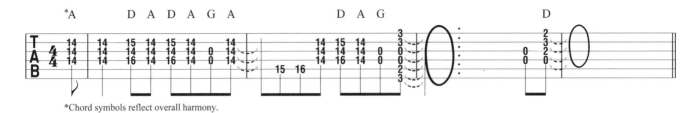

*Chord symbols reflect overall harmony.

"ALL RIGHT NOW"
Words and Music by Andy Fraser and Paul Rodgers

For this banner riff from guitarist Paul Kossoff of Free, we're presenting all eight measures of the intro, but each four-bar take is arranged slightly different. The first four measures are a simplified version, using the I–IV change as you just learned it. The second iteration is exactly how Kossoff played it, with a couple of extra frills like the big open A5 chord to start it, and the cool Dadd4 chord that really gives it that something extra. For the A5, barre the typical open A chord, but add your pinky across strings 2–1 at the fifth fret. For the Dadd4, play the IV-chord shape the way you just learned, but lift your index finger, so the open G string can ring.

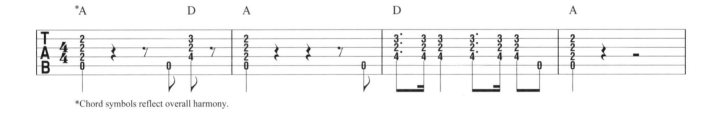

*Chord symbols reflect overall harmony.

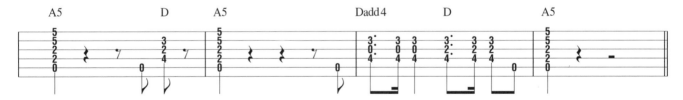

Congratulations! You've reached the end of *Do-It-Yourself: Guitar*, and guess what? You've done it yourself. We can't think of a much better way to celebrate your newfound guitar skills than with one of the greatest rock 'n' roll anthems of all time—"Rock and Roll All Nite" by KISS. This tune features the Keith Richards chord move you just learned, some power-chord 5–6 boogie, and a cool minor pentatonic-based guitar solo. So cue the stage lights, turn up your amp, and get ready to rock and roll all nite and party every day—but be sure to leave plenty of time for practice!

"ROCK AND ROLL ALL NITE"

Words and Music by Paul Stanley and Gene Simmons

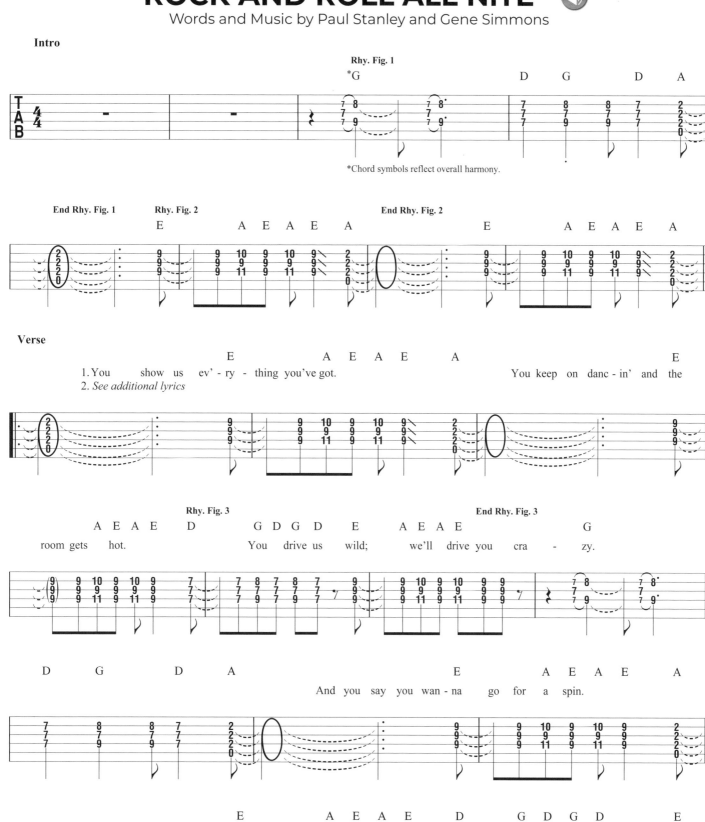

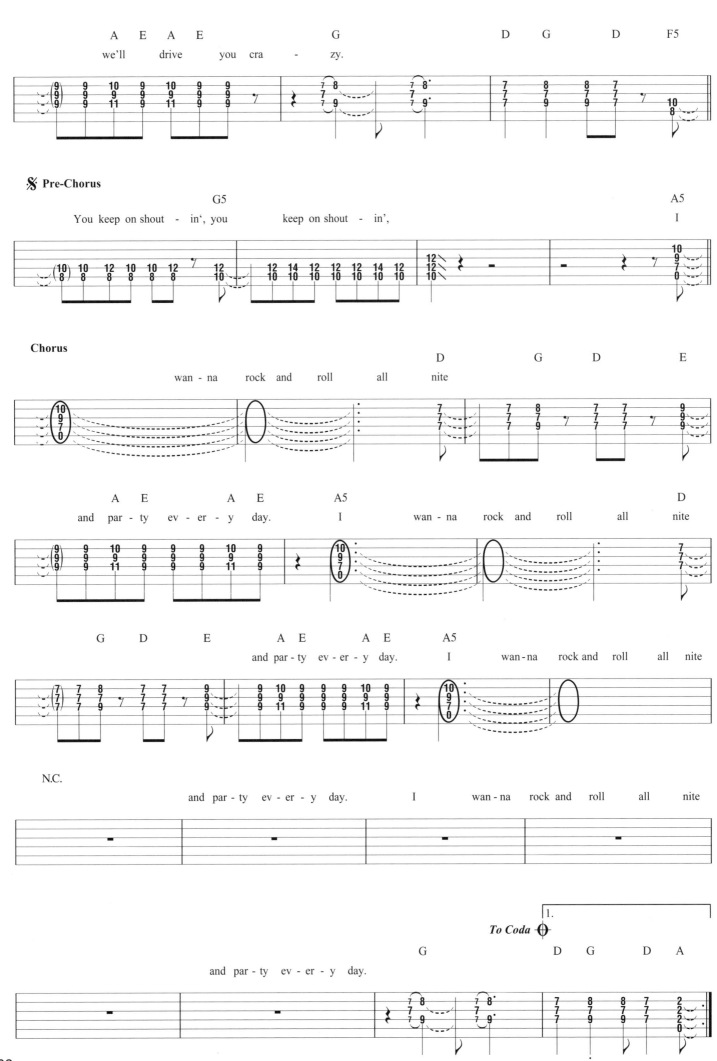

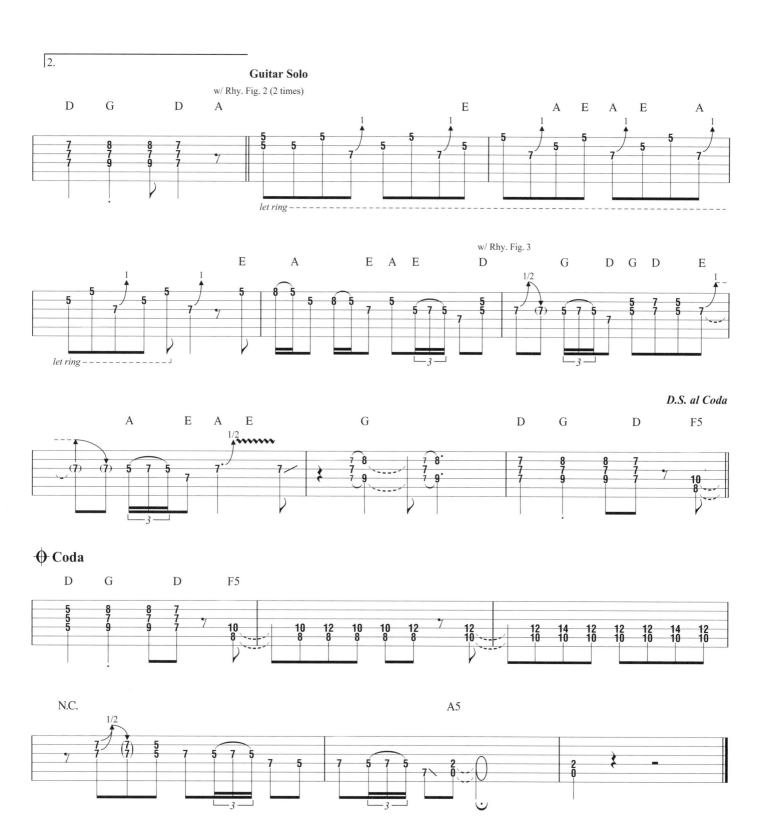

Additional Lyrics

2. You keep on sayin' you'll be mine for a while.
You're looking fancy and I like your style.
And you drive us wild; we'll drive you crazy.
And you show us ev'rything you've got.
Well, baby, baby, that's quite a lot.
And you drive us wild; we'll drive you crazy.

Appendix—
Your Guitar Toolbox

The following pages contain some reference materials you may find helpful as you work through this book and progress in your playing.

Parts of the Guitar

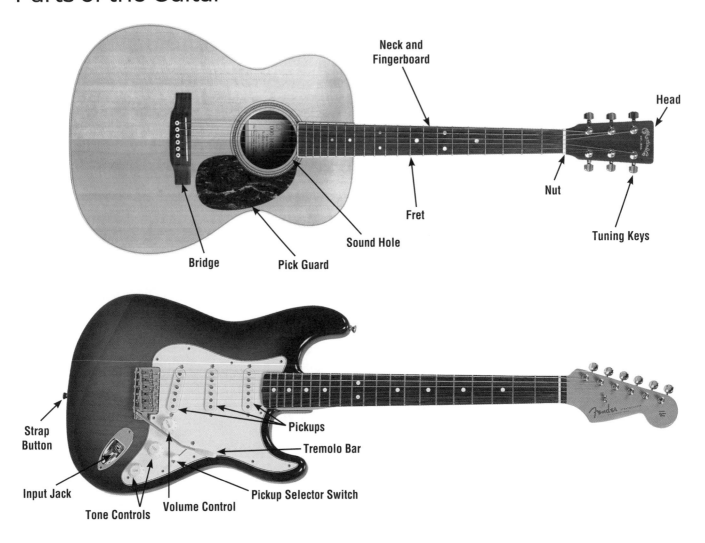

Capo: A sort of mechanical clamp, a capo holds down all six strings at a selected fret. For example, if you place a capo at the third fret and play each string, from low to high, you'll get the following pitches: G, C, F, B♭, D, G. Capos are typically used by singer-songwriters who want to play "cowboy" chords in a different key.

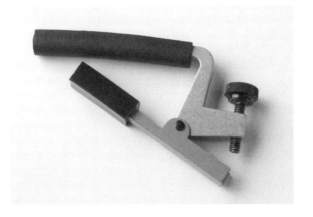

Guitar Talk

Here are definitions and descriptions of the guitar jargon you're likely to hear not only in this book but in other lessons or even just in conversation with other guitarists.

Accidental: When a note outside of a key is played, it's indicated with a sharp (#), flat (♭), or natural (♮) symbol. For example, the key of G has only one sharp note (F#), so if you play C#, it would be an accidental. Likewise, if you played F natural instead of F#, that too would be an accidental.

Alternate Picking: When using a pick, the act of using a fairly strict "down-up-down-up" pattern of picking notes (or, up-down-up-down).

Axe: Another name for "guitar," typically used to describe electric guitars and almost always in a rock or heavy metal context.

Bar: A more colloquial name for "measure."

Blue Note: Technically refers to any note that causes musical tension, but generally is associated with playing the ♭3rd over a major or dominant chord (i.e., playing the minor pentatonic scale over a 7th chord), the ♭7th over a major chord, or the ♭5th as heard in the blues scale.

BPM: An acronym for "beats per minute," which defines the tempo of a song.

Chord Grip: Refers to the specific fingering of a chord.

Cowboy Chords: This term refers to open chords. This nickname came about from the old-time country artists like Roy Rogers and the singing cowboy himself, Gene Autry, who used open chords extensively in their songs.

Double Stops: Refers to two notes played simultaneously, typically in the context of riffs or licks, and most often on adjacent strings.

Fret Hand: Refers to your hand that holds down the strings on the fretboard. Due to the overwhelming prevalence of right-handed guitarists, you'll also hear this frequently referred to simply as your "left hand," though that practice should be avoided.

Interval: The musical distance between two notes. For example, the distance from C to E is a major 3rd, from C to G is a perfect 5th, and C to C is an octave.

Low E String/High E String: Your guitar has two E strings, and the "high" and "low" adjectives refer to the **pitch** of each, rather than its physical orientation. So the "low E string" is actually closer to the sky (higher), but it is lower in pitch. Conversely, the "high E string" is higher in pitch but physically closer to the ground.

Run Your Scales: An informal way of saying practice playing scales by repeatedly playing them in both ascending (low to high) and descending (high to low) directions.

Stompbox: Another name for guitar effect pedals that require you to step, or "stomp," on a button or switch to activate the effect.

Tremolo: This one is tricky, because it can have several meanings. Used in the phrase "tremolo picking," it means to alternately pick (up/down) a note as fast as you can. It can also be used in place of "whammy" when referring to the metal bar that attaches to the bridge on some guitars and, when depressed, lowers the pitch of all ringing strings. Finally, it also is the name of an effect where a note's or chord's amplitude is rapidly changed, achieved via the use of a tremolo effect pedal or sometimes built into an amplifier.

Up the Neck/Down the Neck: The former refers to moving your fret hand from the headstock toward the body of the guitar, typically concurrent with notes higher in pitch. The latter—the opposite— moving your fret hand from the guitar body toward the headstock, typically resulting in lower-pitched notes.

Whammy Bar: A short metal arm that attaches to the bridge of some electric guitars that, when depressed, lowers the pitch of all ringing notes. Some bridges are set up to "float," which in turn allows you to pull up on the whammy bar and thus raise the pitch of any ringing notes.

Fretboard Diagram

Here is a diagram of all the notes in the first 12 frets of your guitar's fretboard, including the open string names. You'll notice that the notes at the 12th fret match the open-string note names. It's at the 12th fret that the notes repeat the pattern, so the 13th-fret notes equal the first-fret notes, 14th-fret notes match second-fret notes, and so on.

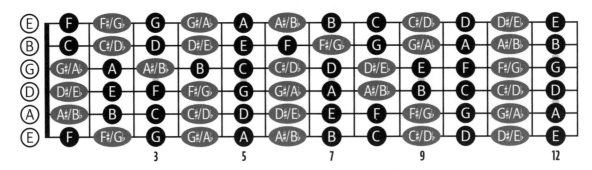

Chord Reference

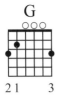
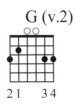

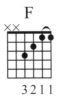

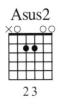
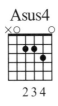
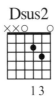
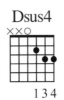

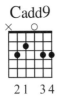
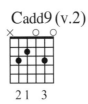

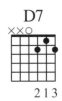

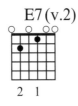

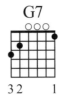
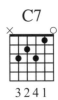

Strum Patterns

Below you'll find the most commonly used strumming patterns. Not all were presented in the book, but they are all used extensively in pop, rock, country, and folk music.

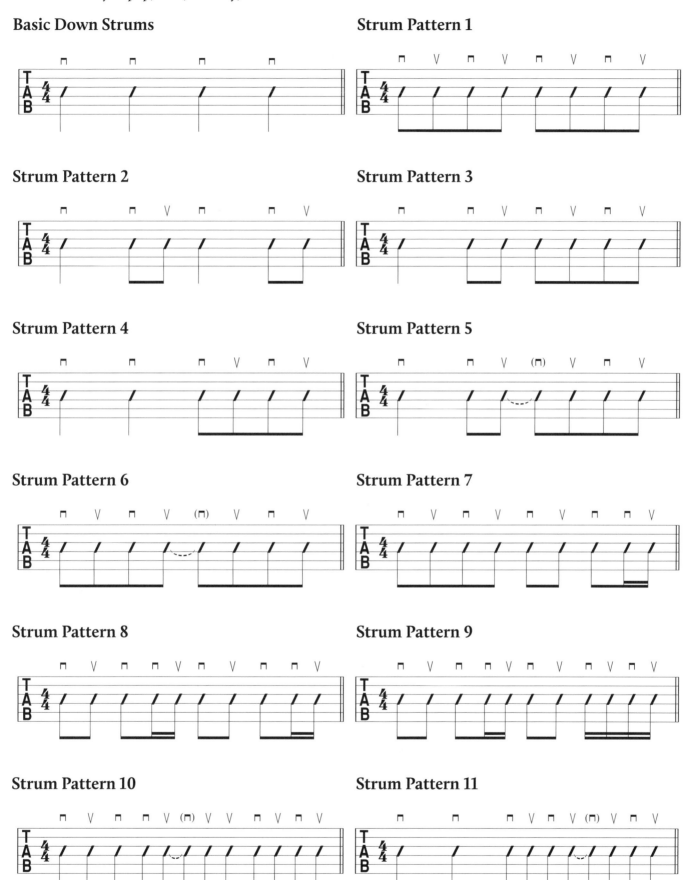

Basic Down Strums

Strum Pattern 1

Strum Pattern 2

Strum Pattern 3

Strum Pattern 4

Strum Pattern 5

Strum Pattern 6

Strum Pattern 7

Strum Pattern 8

Strum Pattern 9

Strum Pattern 10

Strum Pattern 11

About the Author

Michael Mueller is a Nashville-based guitarist and writer. He has written over 20 instructional guitar and music books, including the *Hal Leonard Rock Guitar Method*, the *Hal Leonard Acoustic Tab Method*, the *Hal Leonard Guitar Tab Method* (Book 3), *Scale Chord Relationships*, *100 Rock Guitar Lessons*, and *100 Acoustic Guitar Lessons*, among others. He was formerly the manager of instructional guitar web site *GuitarInstructor.com*, as well as the editor in chief of *Guitar One* magazine, where he conducted video guitar lessons with such iconic guitarists as Joe Satriani, Neal Schon, Eric Johnson, Mark Tremonti, Angus and Malcolm Young, Zakk Wylde, Joe Bonamassa, Vernon Reid, and John 5, among many others. His work has also appeared in *Guitar World*, *Guitar Player*, *Bass Guitar World, Jazz Times*, and Sirius XM.